Table of Contents - Map:

Distinctions in implementations.

But are we free ?

To bootstrap or not.

Finally !

Goodbye for now.

Suggested reading.

Conscious Artificial Intelligence (C.A.i.)
Part I. Foundations

Preface

When I was about 8 years old, my daily routine involved going to school in my native Mexico City, doing the things that a normal school kid does and returning home thoroughly exhausted. The next part of my daily routine usually involved me lounging in the couch while watching cartoons and waiting for my mom to call me for dinner.

On one such occasion, the phone, a landline rotary phone which was on the opposite side of the room started ringing, I stood up to answer it a little too fast and suddenly I was victim to blood rushing down from my head, I fainted on the way to answer it, I blacked out for a few seconds and woke up, the phone still ringing,I answered it a little extra groggy and apparently not much worse for the wear.

I can't remember who it was on the other end of the line (*probably a telemarketer*), but ever since that incident I have been fascinated by the subject of consciousness, specifically what happened to me during those few seconds, I was after all the same person but it was as if I ceased to exist and then promptly resumed existing, much in the same way electrical light does when you flip a switch.

***

Computers entered my life at a very young age, by my recollection I was first exposed to them while visiting my aunt in San Francisco, she worked at a finance company and I was left under her supervision for a few hours, she must have had some work to do and so she tried to keep me busy by booting up an archaic **IBM PC** (*state of the art at that time*) and fired up **PONG**, ever since then I've been hooked, I think I wrote my first program at around 10 and haven't quite stopped with stints in dot-coms and the web, finance, cryptocurrencies and A.I.

Like many books, this one started as a set of notes accumulated during almost a decade of personal research on the subject of consciousness, memory and artificial intelligence, subjects I enjoy working on in my spare time.

I decided to write this book series, since I believe the current state of affairs as they relate to both neuroscience and applied artificial intelligence could use an outside discussion on the topic of consciousness; additionally, a discussion on artificial consciousness is both relevant and needed to advance these fields, something we have set aside for some time and relegated to science fiction, in the end the ultimate justification for the existence of this book is that I find these topics fascinating and their applications profound and capable of changing our lives for the better, a worthy endeavor I believe and one which I hope to share with you.

Eugenio Noyola Leon (Keno)
Mexico City 2018

***

So where to start?, What's the plan ?.
I've decide to break down or divide the subject of Conscious Artificial Intelligence into two or three medium sized books and maybe a final bigger omnibus one, each one is meant to be a standalone product. I opted to do it this way for both the readers convenience and mine.

In this first book I'll try poking the subject of consciousness from different angles and confront it with intelligence both natural and artificial; while on the subject I'll try giving some perspective on the current state of affairs and some nagging issues we haven't quite resolved, things like qualia and general A.i.s By necessity this one reviews and rehashes a lot of already available information and doesn't go into too much detail to allow for a breezy read and inclusive text. (I hope).

A second book will tentatively leave most definitions behind and clumsily start experimenting and prodding from a more practical stance, a 3rd one will deal with more general aspects like future applications, the nature and implications of an Artificially conscious machine and other considerations, in other words if we were to build an artificial consciousness, then what ?

I am fully aware of the risks of planning follow up books, life or death could happen and they could never be written (*at least by me*), I also hope you don't feel cheated by this book, at first I wasn't sure about it's utility as a standalone product, but now after finishing it I believe it is a very necessary stepping stone, in any case rest assured that a lot of love went into it and plenty of insights can be found here.

***

"History is written by the victors." - **Winston Churchill**

Definitions

If you were to open a dictionary and search for the word consciousness, you would likely get one of the following definitions:

- the state of being awake and aware of one's surroundings.

- the awareness or perception of something by a person.

- the fact of awareness by the mind of itself and the world.

As far as day to day use, these definitions work perfectly fine as a means to communicate the subjective experience we all are intimately acquainted with, we know we are conscious because we feel something when we are not sleeping, blacked out or under anesthesia and we share this feeling or perception with others, the first definition is even broad enough to encompass not only humans but animals and artificial beings.

Problems arise from the second definition which takes a human centric approach via the limitation that consciousness is only available to a person, to humans. This is an evolutionary victory and legacy that colors consciousness due to our place in the environment as the writers of history. So far we've only written history for us, if we were writing for another species, an equal or superior one, we might change our story, we might change our tune.

Until very recently we have also not extended this definition to animals, in part due to ignorance and in part because it has been convenient. Accepting that some or all animals are conscious conflicts with our predatory nature, our morality and our religious & political views.

The third definition brings about a new difficulty in that it presupposes we all have a clear understanding of what the mind is and what awareness is, yet like with consciousness itself we are all in agreement that we do have a mind and that we are aware.

The problem with definitions

Like with other dictionary definitions, there is only so much we can gain from them since they are tools for communication; take for instance the definition of flight:

- The action or process of flying through the air.

This definition unfortunately does not give us any insight into how to build a flying machine or the laws of aerodynamics.

Like with flight, if our goal is to better understand and to emulate or even create new forms of consciousness, we need to look elsewhere and dig deeper.

***

Having somehow exhausted the dictionary, it is now time to see what science and religion have to say about consciousness, remember we are trying to get more information into the inner workings to later try and construct our own artificial consciousness, or at least size the problem and place the first foundational bricks, even if mostly theory, so we need all the help we can get.

RELIGION. You could easily discount religion as a poor source of insights on the subject of consciousness, you might be partially right, but I believe you will also be missing something valuable, perhaps even critical.

Religion and spirituality loom large over the topic, religion is and has been our go to answer to explain consciousness and related phenomena like death, qualia and inner speech, I can even argue with you that our need to explain consciousness and the mind both explain religion and in part consciousness itself.A mind or construct that can ask itself questions about it's environment can ask where does the mind or construct comes from, and religion, absent a clear maker is one answer.

So what does religion have to say about the subject ?

Popular religions of the past and present usually consist of a god, gods or narrative responsible for creation, a story to justify our time alive and an afterlife or process that occurs when we cease to be conscious in the here and now, the common thread here are stories we tell ourselves an others based on anecdotal evidence, stories told by the elders, ancient text and interpretations of these texts and so far it has proven to be a uniquely human activity.

Consciousness is then explained by religion as a property granted by the divine or the universe, perhaps a gift from the gods ?

"Religion is a rich species game"

The earliest signs of religion appear to be burial related (around

40,000 BCE), our ancestors probably started the practice as a sanitary or practical one, and it's not a far fetched hypothesis to say that the memory of the death (exemplified by burial figurines, perhaps dear Ugg that killed a mammoth) followed, from there we see a progressive evolution of religion as a means to explain nature and human life with ever more complex stories and rituals.

The takeaway here is that in species terms we had to achieve some level of mastery of our environment coupled with a certain degree of intelligence for religion to arise, we can then say that various degrees of consciousness mingled with intelligence generated the correct set of circumstances for us to invent religion. Religion in turn allowed us to answer questions our higher consciousness and intelligence might have pondered.

"What would life look like if we were all in agreement that there is no afterlife and that the mind can be explained ?"

Before leaving Religion, it is also worth mentioning how successful and useful an invention it has been, for better or worse most of our species believes to a certain degree that when we cease to be conscious at the end of our life we are recreated or enjoy some sort of afterlife, and that the mind can be explained by concepts like the soul, which we take on faith; purpose in life can also be achieved by following a religion's rules, emulating the divine or playing along some divine plan with certain degree of autonomy, this is an efficient arrangement that has both it's pros and cons, on one end it has allowed us to thrive by ignoring the consequences of our actions and allowed us to focus on expanding while giving us peace of mind about our identity, origin and destiny; on the other hand it has molded our political, social, moral, economic and scientific reach, not always in a benevolent or progressive way.

This is the best we have come up with; by necessity we will have to come up with something better if we wish to replace traditional religion with a modern one that perhaps uses science at it's core.

For instance, this book series argues that consciousness can be explained in scientific, specific terms, as such it brings about some sobering conclusions, mainly that when consciousness ceases, we cease to exist in any meaningful way, a religion that took into account this finding would probably give more importance to life due to the lack of an afterlife.

We will have to leave further considerations for later, this is after all just an overview and introduction, let us now move to a sampling of what science has to offer on the subject.

***

SCIENCE

I like to think that science is the counterpart of religion in the same way that intelligence is popularly considered the counterpart of emotion, we probably need both for a healthy existence, but so far science has been a few steps behind religion in explaining consciousness, in part because of the difficulty, and in part perhaps due to the fragmentation and organization of science itself.

It is perhaps telling and a little surprising that science has yet to come to an agreement as to what consciousness is, how exactly does it work and well, explain it in simple irrefutable terms, yet at the same time there is a lot of constituent parts and insight dispersed across specific fields which we'll sample now, this will unfortunately not be an exhaustive, historic or even correct overview, but rather a curated one based on why I perceive to be some useful foundational parts we can steal for our project of understanding and artificially recreating consciousness, please consult the suggested bibliography at the end of this book for more.

***

BIOLOGY & PHYSICS.

Biology has been hard at work explaining life and the foundational elements of it. Cell biology in particular gives us the valuable insights that living things are made of cells and go through the process of creation, existence, reproduction and death; along with contributions from physics, then we have a clear building ladder composed of atoms, elements and molecules, which in turn are assembled into cells organized via DNA strands which serve as dynamic templates for life, organisms that are embedded into time and space and do certain things in a certain order.

While consciousness is a higher level property of organisms, it is still bound to biology and physics, so it can be explained as an emergent property of matter that is arranged in a specific way after a number of processes occurring through time.

Time, space and consciousness.

Time and space can be thought of as the canvas or background into which consciousness exists, time (for practical purposes) can be defined as that which can be measured by a clock in discrete units, and is crucial for consciousness as rhythms and cycles seem to be integral parts of both life and the cognitive processes behind consciousness as we will later review.

Space itself can have several definitions and properties depending on the scale and domain we are looking into, that is it can be a dimension and can be relativistic, or can be be discrete and fixed.

As it pertains to our discussion, it helps to use the discrete and fixed definitions (although consciousness might still be bound to the dimensional and relativistic aspects), more importantly, rather than get bogged down in the details of how space and matter behave at the quantum level or how time and space are related, we can simply employ them as known elements for now. So an artificial consciousness could be created using software or hardware timers and clocks and can react and exist in either real or virtual space and time or some combination, we'll come back repeatedly to the subject of time throughout our investigation.

***

EVOLUTION.

There is scant evidence that consciousness is a requirement for a species to thrive in this planet, bacteria, trees and insects seem to be doing just fine without the sort of higher consciousness humans and other animals seem to enjoy. It is also unclear if they will outlast us in the evolutionary tree.

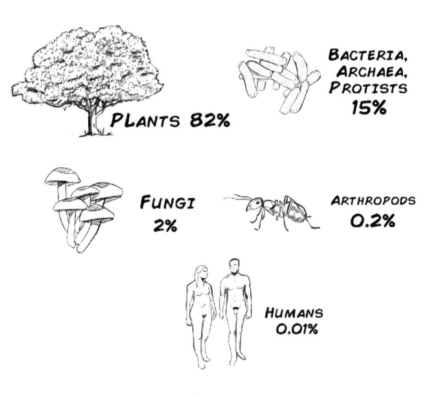

PLANTS 82%

BACTERIA, ARCHAEA, PROTISTS 15%

FUNGI 2%

ARTHROPODS 0.2%

HUMANS 0.01%

Percentage of life on planet earth measured by estimated biomass; Not pictured:

Fish - 0.12%, Mollusks & Cnidarians-0.06%, Annelids & Nematodes-0.04%, Viruses-0.04%, Livestock-0.02%, Wild Mammals-0.001%, Wild Birds-0.0004%. The numbers have changed through the years, but we've always been a small portion. *Current source: Yinon M. Bar-On et al. (2018) The biomass distribution on Earth*

Consciousness (*at least what we sometimes call the higher consciousness of humans*) might or might not be the key to our successful run as species and perhaps more pressing it could be a dead evolutionary end, these are interesting subjects, but unfortunately we need to be sidestep them for now so we can focus on the basics.

It is said that nothing in biology makes sense unless it is seen through the eyes of evolution.

If we wish to recreate an understand consciousness, it is helpful to know how and when it arose, in this regard evolution's contribution in the form of evolutionary & comparative neuroscience should give us the most insights.

For instance, if we were to divide the human brain by functions and regions, we could trace back prototypical structures along with their functions to marine and amphibian species, that is structures involved with sensing and reacting to the environment, maintaining the organism and even higher forms of behavior like memory, sleep, socialization and reproductive behavior which can be found in the brains and nervous systems of species as ancient and basic as fish and worms.

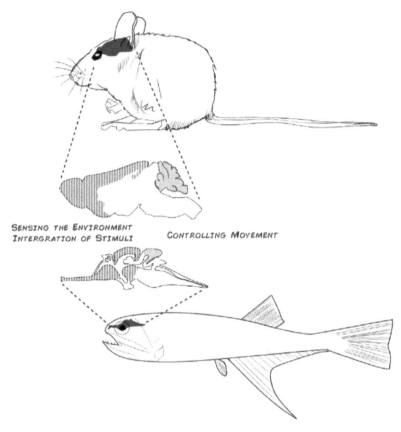

SENSING THE ENVIRONMENT
INTERGRATION OF STIMULI   CONTROLLING MOVEMENT

Comparing the brains of a common rodent (*wood mouse*) and a common fish (*Bristlemouth*).

But why this complexity?, well, if you subscribe to the evolutionary theory of natural selection, consciousness contributes to the organism in some way which gives it a greater probability to survive and reproduce. The competing theory being that it is just a byproduct of other evolutionary or even random adaptations or changes in DNA.

When precisely this happened and in which species is hard to pinpoint due to the lack of specifics and as we will briefly cover the lack of clear boundaries... what precisely do we mean by consciousness as it relates to biological systems ? take for instance plants, which as we mentioned might be the most successful beings on this planet, plants can sense the environment, communicate with each other and to a certain degree can have memory of certain environmental conditions, so we would have to go back 470 million years and trace these evolutions in plants and other beings, if on the other hand we start higher up with our immediate predecessors in the evolutionary tree, the story is somehow easier to digest.

The primate (and later human) brain in particular seem to be an addition of adaptations showing an increase in size and specialization in certain areas, but across many other species (fish, reptiles, mammals, insects, birds)   there exist similar core structures and networks which serve the same purposes, so it's not too far a jump to make the reasonable assumption that other species experience consciousness, albeit a different kind derived by their specific adaptations, where one draws the line depends in great part on what definition of consciousness and worldview one has.

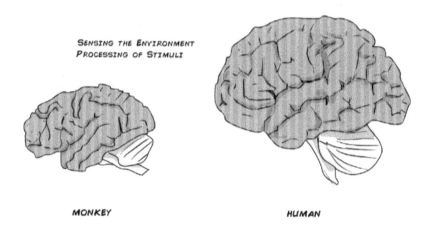

SENSING THE ENVIRONMENT
PROCESSING OF STIMULI

MONKEY   HUMAN

A popular evolutionary analogy is that of the brain as a house, rather than a predesigned structure, rooms have been added or expanded over time to our house as our specific needs have evolved, some have been reused, share disparate functions and some due to their very recent addition are in a less than ideal place, it's as if evolution is simply throwing things at the wall to see what sticks, rather than a thoughtful artisan with a plan building something from scratch.

My contribution to this analogy is to think about consciousness as the light inside the house, in early houses there were candles that barely lit the rooms, but in later additions the need for bright lights at all times required new connections, cabling and changed the energy requirements, we can also look across the road to other species houses and while they might not all be bright in the same way as ours, they also have light in them.

At this point it is also useful to start thinking about degrees of consciousness; a plant, fungi or insect is aware of it's environment, so in some way it is conscious, when you wake up in the morning you are aware of your surroundings, yet this consciousness is different from the one you experience while thinking, experiencing an emotion, writing or solving a problem; consciousness as we will later see seems to be an integration of systems and not an unitary standalone process, so as a first pass we can grossly think of degrees of consciousness in species through time as related to number and size of systems devoted to processing external and internal stimuli from the environment and itself.

This point needs to be examined a little closer, different brain networks and systems acting together or in sequence produce different states of consciousness, awareness of the self, awareness of the environment, awareness of others, creation and manipulation of ideas, recollection of memories and a myriad of other processes, yet we normally group them together under a few descriptive definitions, or simply consciousness...

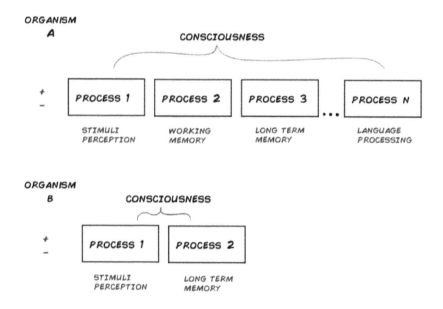

In this schema, organism A is perceiving 2 environmental stimuli, it could be the strong scent of vanilla and faint cold temperature, by holding them in working memory for a little while, the long term memory of Grandma baking Vanilla cookies in winter could pop out and be communicated.

Organism B, A rodent perceives the scent of cheese and the slight movement of giant creatures nearby, long term memory informs the rodent that he needs to wait till there is no movement to get the deliciously smelling thing.

Both organisms are conscious or are experiencing a conscious moment, yet their individual nature and circumstances are different.

A big part of understanding consciousness and a good plan of attack revolves around differentiating these processes, listing them in detail and examining them; we'll revisit this subject and start figuring out what processes are involved in later sections.

***

MEDCINE.

Anesthesia

Consciousness can be suspended medically to avoid awareness of a medical operation (*the medical term is hypnosis*), this suspension can be maintained and then later resumed more or less on command, usually with little to no consequences. One would think that an anesthesiologist then has the final word on consciousness, unfortunately that is not his job, that is he is not tasked with explaining consciousness, but rather suspending it temporarily in a safe way, but the insights are still there for us to profit.

The reason for this apparent lack of inner knowledge has in part to do with the history of anesthesia and the complex nature of the brain.

The History part is simple to explain, for thousand of years humans have been ingesting a variety of substances and recording their effects, some have been toxic, some nutritious and some have altered consciousness, a few have interrupted it in a forced sleep kind of way. This last category has been helpful for dealing with disease and medical procedures, and so we rather stumbled on the discovery that consciousness can be interrupted and altered by ingesting certain substances.

A brief and incomplete list of substances that have served as anesthetics inducing loss of consciousness would read as follows:

- Alcohol
- Opium
- Ether
- Nitrous Oxide
- Chloroform
- Sevoflurane
- Propofol
- Ketamine

The exact mechanism by which the above work is poorly understood in detail, but there is evidence that they all work by disrupting the integration of information in the brain, a valuable insight; let's look a little closer.

Propofol is currently (along with Ketamine) a widely used general anesthetic for starting and maintaining general anesthesia used mostly in surgery, but you might be more familiar with Sevoflurane or a similar gas which is inhaled while at the dentist and provokes you to loose consciousness in a matter of seconds and then allows the dentists to do some work on you without you experiencing anything.

A few years back I had some dental work done under general anesthesia, the experience is a little unsettling but fascinating if you are into consciousness; an anesthesiologist places a breathing mask on you and asks you to count backwards from 10, I remember maybe reaching 7 before loosing consciousness, after that it is as if black bar was placed during the following hour or so, I have no recollection of what happened in that time period or even the notion that time had passed and experienced no pain or sensations, the next thing I remember is being awoken with numbness in my mouth and being somehow groggy, these effects dissipated during the next few hours and I was back to normal.

The mechanisms of action of general anesthetics like sevoflurane and propofol are not entirely understood, but they are believed to act as agonists on GABAA receptors in the brain, a sentence that will make little to no sense if you are not a neuroscientist, but don't worry, we'll delve into the details later.

For now, a simplistic explanation would be as follows:

The brain is composed of individual computational units called neurons which communicate via action potentials, receptors in neurons act as modulated gateways for action potentials, the modulation is usually either inhibitory (less action potentials) or excitatory (more action potentials), consciousness is believed to work by the integration of activity in various regions of the brain, this integration is modulated by neuron receptors in specific areas, so by artificially amplifying the inhibitory effects of GABAA receptors (the agonist part) the communication in between areas is temporarily suspended and you loose consciousness.

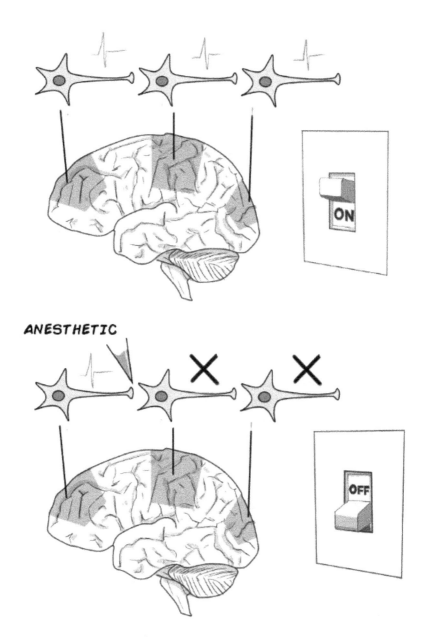

Simplified mechanism of proposed anesthetic action, the closest we have to an on/off switch for consciousness.

Armed with this brief bit of knowledge, let's review what happened to me:

Before being placed under general anesthesia I was aware of my environment, a number of networks in my brain were active, the regions in my brain in charge of the senses were processing the environment and I was aware I was at the dentist, neurons were firing and some were integrating the experience into a cohesive whole I experienced as being conscious.

In the few seconds during which I was inhaling Sevoflurone, certain neurons went into overdrive blocking the messaging in between areas, this areas involved mainly memory and perception but for the most part left autonomic functions like breathing and cardiac functions alone.

During the dental procedure, communication in between areas was blocked as long as the administration of the anesthetic (the maintenance period) continued, it is important to note that even though the integration of information was interrupted, individual areas might still be active, so some part of my brain might have registered the pain, but since the whole of my brain never experienced it or I remember it, to me (*the integrator*) at least it never happened.

Coming out of anesthesia involved ceasing the administration of the anesthetic, with some other anesthetics or procedures, other substances might need to be administered, but in my case the gas just wore off and the previously blocked pathways started talking again, swiftly recreating a new reality in which I had access to my previous awareness of arriving to the dentist and my new one of having numbness, grogginess and that I had went under some dental procedure.

A couple of takeaways from anesthesia:

Consciousness can be interrupted, the mechanisms are not entirely understood in detail, but it's believe they involve network inhibition, consciousness is an integration of information across brain regions and networks.

21

***

Consciousness & Disease.

Medicine possesses an intimate knowledge about consciousness, like with other specializations in science, it has a singular focus which is disease or injury, so it is mostly interested in evaluating or diagnosing states of consciousness and how they signify any underlying malfunction, condition or deviation from the norm as well as which structures are involved and of course how to treat them to return them to a normal state.

In order to evaluate medical degrees of consciousness or lack of it, a variety of scales have been developed, once more there is ample overlap and difference in between them, but following is a brief summary, note that these scales start from a simple baseline or baselines and has a medical focus, so it can be considered incomplete for our final purpose of understanding consciousness, but serves as another set of valuable insights into the inner workings.

In General, we can summarize medical scales of consciousness in 3 broad categories:

1. Normal or baseline consciousness states.

2. Impaired consciousness states.

3. A lack of consciousness state.

Let's go through them one by one:

Normal or baseline consciousness states.

In a normal state of consciousness, you are aware of your

environment, maybe you are in a coffeeshop writing a book, you are focused on writing the next paragraph, so you think about various things you want to mention and mull them over before writing them down on your computer or notebook, at the same time you notice things like the flavor and temperature of your coffee, the couple at the table next to you and other environmental details, but you can switch back and forth in between tasks at will, you are also alert to unexpected things like a drink falling from the table next to you.

There are other elements to this medically normal state of consciousness, for instance, most include sleep and periods of grogginess, if you were to become a little tired after writing that paragraph and decided to take a nap, you would experience a period of less consciousness and a break from it, but for medical purposes everything would be normal.

Additionally, other regions of your body are acting normally, specifically your autonomic nervous system is taking care of the internal business of running a human body, a mammoth task you are thankfully barely aware off.

Impaired consciousness states.

While I hope you never experience an impaired state of consciousness tied to a disease, chances are you already have, or at least a very similar one:

You stayed until very very late working on your book, sometime in between the hours of 1am and 2am you decided to have some Whisky to help the creative process, and somewhere around 4am you decided to call it a night, you almost forgot, you have an important meeting tomorrow at 7am, so you set your alarm for just a couple of hours of sleep, what awaits when you wake up is an impaired state of consciousness we usually call sleep deprivation or a hangover when there is alcohol involved, you will unfortunately have both.

Among the symptoms you might experience are inattention, grogginess and difficulty piecing together ideas or doing anything complex, your short term memory can also be impaired, you can't hold on to any new information let alone consult something from the past, yet it also seems that some brain processes have taken a life of their own, a catchy song you heard last night keeps on repeating in some part of your brain, you are grumpy or feeling silly for no apparent reason, you might speak with a bit of a slur and you really really want to go back to bed and sleep some more.

Things wouldn't be that bad for you if you weren't also really dehydrated and had a headache, these 2 symptoms are usually due to the toxicity of alcohol, so in a strict sense just try imagining all of the above, but without this added insult. It is also worth noting that an impaired state of consciousness can manifest itself in other ways, it can be of an intermittent nature and more gravely can intensify to dangerous levels, take for instance grogginess or lack of wakefulness, at one end you could be slightly inconvenienced, but at the other you will be unable to move or react to the environment or others and you would eventually perish.

In general the more you are unresponsive to internal or external stimuli the worse off you are in medically conscious terms, additionally there is often some correlation in between how unresponsive you are and the biological structures that are suffering damage, we will use this insight while delving into the nuts and bolts of consciousness & related structures later.

Lack of consciousness.

At the far end of the impaired or diminished conscious states lies a situation where you would be unresponsive to the environment, external and internal stimuli, importantly unlike some deep sleep states, you would also be unarousable, not even painful stimuli could wake you up, you would unfortunately be in a **coma**, the medical term given to this state; like with all the previous states there is a scale of severity, this one involves the amount of brain activity, currently measured by electrical activity and again is a rough reflection of how dispersed the damage is as well as affected structures in the brain.

How does a coma feel? That is a tough question to answer, anecdotal evidence from patients that have undergone a coma, either report a complete black bar and no recollection of events for the duration or sleep like dreams and hallucinations, the more common one being repeating dreams and even some limited awareness of their situation or external stimuli. We'll get into the thorny details of inner experiences later, but suffice is to say that depending on the lesions and individual patient, some awareness of external or internal stimuli might persist during a coma, even if intermittent.

At the far end of a coma (a deep coma), brain activity is almost non existent, yet your autonomic system keeps on working, your body is alive although it needs external help to remain alive and you are not conscious in any meaningful way, the black bar never ending...

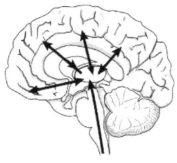

NORMAL, BASELINE

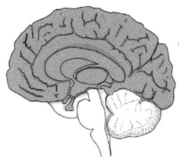

CONFUSION, INDIFFERENCE DROWSINESS, STUPOR, LAPSES INTO SLEEP

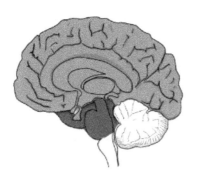

NON RESPONSIVE, EVEN TO DEEP PAIN, FLACID,

Affected regions of the brain and their related level of consciousness, note the integrative region in the middle of the normal working brain, (the thalamus) and it's projections to outer areas (cortical regions).

Brain Death.

Beyond a deep coma lies brain death, which is loosely defined as lack of electrical activity in the brain and a lack of blood flow, but the ultimate definition is that it is irreversible for now, no one has come back from brain death, although it's not out of the realm of possibilities that one day we will know how, after all stroke and other medical conditions were once thought to be unsurmountable.

The biggest takeaway from this whirlwind tour of medical consciousness
is that once again consciousness seems to be an integrative and gradual affair, that is there is no definitive on/off switch or even a single proof of consciousness as generally defined, but rather a range of conscious behavior tied to specific networks and brain structures along with their level of activity, there is also precious insights on the quality of a degraded consciousness be it a hangover or coma and ultimately the nature of biological consciousness in the form of electrical activity, biological structures, systems and networks; the specifics unsurprisingly come from the field of neuroscience which we will sample soon.

***

The human purview of consciousness & awareness.

It is remarkable how much of researching any given subject is subtracting our human nature and preconceptions, they are after all part of our history and makeup, man made ideas and distortions abound in science, take for instance this seemingly random division right here in between medicine and neuroscience & psychology, the concepts of life, free will, justice ,good and bad, you get the idea. In this brief section straddling other sections I would like to explore the basic nature of consciousness and awareness via some practical observations hopefully devoid of as many man made ideas as possible…

Let's rewind a bit to the start of this book when I briefly mentioned I fainted on my way to pick up the phone, the experience of anesthesia, deep sleep or coma could also serve as examples. In describing these types of events to others a black bar signifying lack of stimuli seems like a reasonable place to start:

A description then of that faithful afternoon would visually look like this:

Extending this symbolism to our full lives gives us a new perspective:

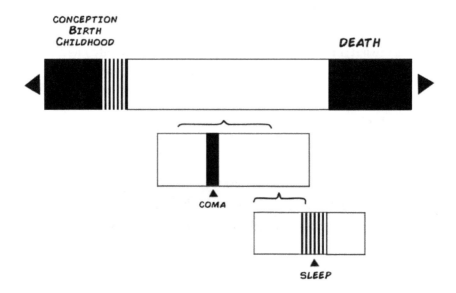

*Here we have a highly compressed but interesting view of someones life, let's say he/
she lived for 85 years, and had a week long coma after an accident midway through life
(graphic in the middle), the last graph exemplifies a day and the intermittent nature of
consciousness while asleep. Notice that during childhood consciousness gradually
emerged, but abruptly ended upon death, something quite common, although not unique.*

And ultimately extending it to a species or universal scale gives us
some needed humility:

EARTH 4.5 BILLION YRS

PLANTS,FUNGI ▶

DINOSAURS ▶

◀ MAN

Conscious or aware beings have been part of this planet for only a fraction of it's life, we don't know if this is common or even if there are other places where this happens, we also know we humans have only been part of it for a very small amount of time.

The first important distortion here is the seemingly innocent black bar, we are extremely visual beings and a lot of mental real estate is devoted to that function alone, but a child that is born blind does not cease to experience consciousness, nor does an animal without a visual system, so the black bar is just a result of our limited communication tools here on paper or screen and my choice of metaphor, the black bar then needs you the reader to also understand that it symbolizes a lack of other stimuli like sound, touch, smell etc, etc:

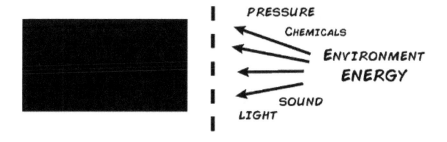

Interestingly if you were to list all the things we or other beings can experience from the environment, they all seem to have something to do with energy (waves, particles), so an even more metaphysical definition of consciousness might deal with the ability to perceive and interact with energy and matter.

Our second distortion is that by trying to explain consciousness to others, I immediately restrict the truth, (*whatever that might be*) to the capacity of those in the audience, so I can't explain it to other conscious beings unless we share the same conscious experience or can somehow translate ours to theirs, in the reverse case a higher or different conscious being would have an equally hard time explaining their experience to us.

More human made distortions exist, for instance, the bookends of existence and consciousness (and even some middle or intermittent parts like sleep) seem to be identical from the outside, even more at scale, yet we don't think much about them in these terms, by and large the period of time before we exist and are born and that after our life have a different quality than the anesthesia session, just ask religion.

Scale is another distortion here, consciousness and awareness both seem to straddle the ms time period for immediate things and longer spans in the minutes, hours, etc for longer timespans, yet if I were to ask you were you conscious or aware this last year ? your response would be the same as if I had asked you about the last minute or second, complicating things further, spatial and temporal ranges outside our biological experience are for the most part unknown, that is we know there are other scales, but we simply don't know much about consciousness in those ambits; speaking about time, notice that to the subject (me) the jump from being conscious to unconscious and back to conscious was immediate, time ceased to be observed, but to an outsider it was not, it follows then that consciousness is a subjective phenomenon, rather than an objective one.

Once we remove all these man made concepts and limits what remains ?

Well, there is a universe that might or might not be infinite, it is full of things (matter & energy) in some parts and mostly empty in others, it also has different scales, both temporal and spatial.

Consciousness, (or awareness if you prefer) on the other hand seems to be a very sporadic (to both the individual, species and even planet scales) phenomenon, so far we believe it happens at a narrow temporal and spatial range, it's a fast eroding island (or archipelago if you count other beings), surrounded by a sea of darkness and nothingness, and last but not least the phenomenon itself seems to consist of a temporary and arbitrary witnessing of the universe, or the witnessing of entropy through information if you will.

31

While these considerations might not be immediately relevant, it is of some comfort to know we can come back to this simple point of view if we stray too far or loose focus.

With that out of the way, let's pick up where we left off.

***

NEUROSCIENCE & PSYCHOLOGY

The brain is one of the most complex things we humans have dealt with; neuroscience, the branch of science in charge of its study is in turn quite a complex thing; the brain has also proven to be inaccessible in a number of ways, at least with our current tools. As mentioned previously this book series is meant to break modest ground, and so for our purposes we will need to summarize established knowledge and derive from it, the details and history are better explained elsewhere.

I've opted to combine psychology and neuroscience in this section due to the overlap in concepts, functions and behavior as they pertain to consciousness, I see both camps as equal contributors for our goal of understanding and recreating consciousness artificially and both have contributed enormously to the subject, you can also think of this section as neuropsychology.

Subject matter.

Our basic biological function, like most living things in this planet is to survive and reproduce, as such, the bulk of our biology is devoted to dealing with stimuli both external and internal which subserve these goals, a series of evolutionary adaptations has produced an organism that is grossly divided into a sensory system, a motor system for sensing and interacting with the environment and the self, and a stimuli processing system that coordinates both, in most animals this arrangement is called a nervous system, this is of course a simplistic view; multiple other systems exist that could be considered parallel (like homeostasis) or complementary & overlapping (like memory, sleep, and many cognitive functions).

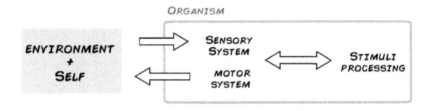

Nervous systems.

The overarching theme in nervous systems amongst animals is a division of labor, roughly speaking there are sensory cells that provide feedback to the organism about the environment and itself, processing cells that evaluate said input, motor cells that allow the organism to interact with the environment or the self and connecting cells in between them that carry information back and forth, this division in vertebrates is divided into a Central Nervous System (**CNS**) comprised by the brain and the spinal cord (connections and processing) and a Peripheral Nervous System (**PNS**) comprised of nerves that either receive information from the environment (*called sensory or afferent*) or transmit information from the brain (*called efferent or motor*).

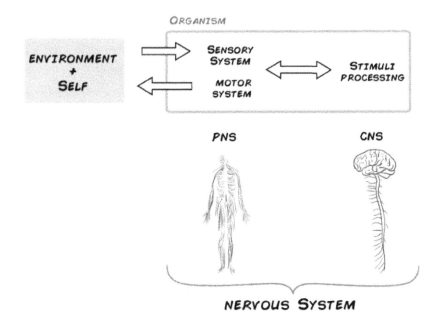

***

Behold the brain...

At the very top of the central nervous system in humans, mammals and other animals lies the brain, we'll focus on the human one for now; as mentioned the brain's main purpose is the processing of environmental and internal stimuli out of which consciousness is thought to arise, not least important though are self regulation and homeostasis related functions which mostly lie outside of our scope, but obviously are of great importance for survival and evolutionary purposes.

At around 3 lbs (or 1.3 kgs) the brain accounts for roughly 2% of our bodies weight and consumes around 20% of the energy our body produces, if you were to extract one out of a skull and the protective outer layers you would end up with a mix of blood and blood vessels which serve to nourish cells, cerebrospinal fluid which serves as a flotation and homeostatic device and a pale brown wrinkled and complex mass with the consistency of soft tofu which constitutes the brain proper.

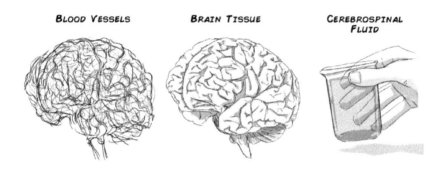

BLOOD VESSELS   **BRAIN TISSUE**   **CEREBROSPINAL FLUID**

Beyond certain differences in color (darker, grayish or lighter beige areas), this mass can prove to be pretty homogenous to the naked eye, in order to extract more information and differences we would need to move to the microscope.

Upon closer inspection, the brain tissue is mostly comprised of 3 types of elements: neurons, axons and glia cells…

Glia cells (or Neuroglia) are supportive cells that attend to neurons and provide a host of functions like axon myelination (for fast communication), neuron positioning, inhibition and other important housekeeping functions like providing nutrients, oxygen and defending against pathogens, while neurons as we will see have a language all of their own, neuroglia seem to affect and support this communication according to the bodies state to a certain degree, when healthy they promote it and when injured they decrease and fence off compromised neurons. Two more interesting facts about glia: by volume they account for about half of the brain, pathology (or disease) involving glia is poorly understood, but it seems to play roles in autism, Parkinson's, depression and other conditions.

What remains after peeling away all these elements are neurons, the computational elements of the brain and their axons & dendrites which respectively serve as communication elements for sending and receiving information, most of the remaining discussion will center into the specifics of these elements and how they arrange themselves into medium and larger sized systems with specific functions, but before getting there, we need to step back and take a look at how they group themselves at a macro level, a first pass at functional division.

A tale of 3 or 4 Brains...

Starting from the bottom up, the brain stem and overlapping structures can be considered the entry, exit, distribution and modulation points for stimuli and motor functions originating from peripheral sensory and motor neurons relayed through the spinal cord, the brain stem can then be considered a hub or relay station that roughly divides the informational system of the brain in 2, on one end the Cerebellum & Cerebrum which process stimuli and motor functions and on the other one the sensory input and motor controls. Another way of thinking about the significance and function is through injury; at the extreme, brain stem stroke causes locked-in syndrome (LIS), a condition in which you would be unable to move any muscle, so you wouldn't be able to communicate ,yet be aware and retain sensation, other more localized injuries also affect sensation, levels of awareness and importantly consciousness, this area is also in charge of basic autonomic functions like sleep/wake cycles, cardiovascular and respiratory control and plays a role in excitation, motivation and habituation, as previously mentioned when total failure happens the result is an unresponsive state we call coma.

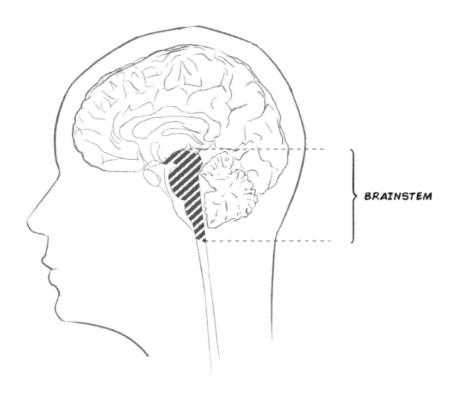

BRAINSTEM

Towards the back of the brain stem lies the cerebellum, a mini brain of sorts whose function involves fine motor control and motor learning, but is also related to timing and other cognitive functions, importantly it is believed that movement is not initiated in the cerebellum, but only controlled by it in detail as it relates to sensory feedback. Once more it is perhaps more revealing to see what happens when it fails due to injury or disease; depending on which part or the cerebellum is incapacitated, your capacity to balance yourself while walking could be diminished, your would be able to start movement, but would overshoot your destination or misjudge your strength, in general you would have problems using and coordinating your muscles and movement as they relate to the outside world.

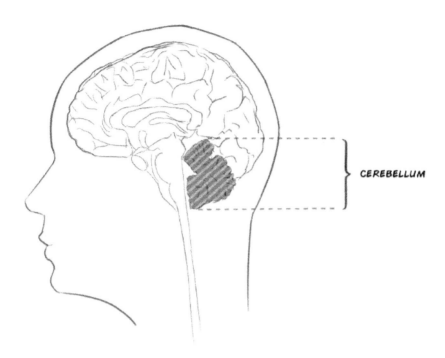

CEREBELLUM

Moving up… on top of the brain stem and cerebellum lies a set of structures that constitute the limbic system; the limbic system is believed to have important roles in memory formation, recall and emotion creation and control, additionally, it serves as a connection and relay hub for the cerebrum or cortex where higher processing takes place; along with the cerebrum/cortex it is of particular interest for the study of consciousness due to its position in the integrative whole, a prime candidate for the seat of consciousness, or at least the copilot; injury or disease to the limbic system affects memory formation and recall as well as a varied number of emotional and cognitive related distortions.

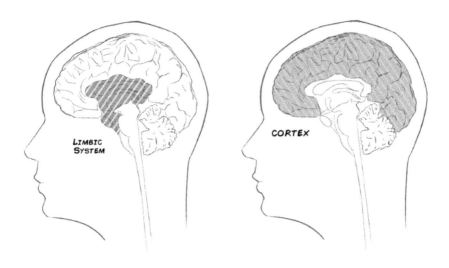

Note: The cerebrum usually contains the limbic system or some parts of it and the cortex, and is usually the 3rd and final division of the brain in some literature, I think dividing it into 4 parts might serve us better for now...

Arriving at the top and final part of the brain we encounter the cortex, which is the folded larger mass you might be familiar with, structurally the cortex consist of a thin outer layer of neurons or grey mater and the axonal myelinated tracts or white matter, functionally the cortex itself is organized around the sensory information received from the lower brain structures and derives functions via processing and interplay with this and other areas across the cortex. A detailed examination of each one of these interactions, whether they affect consciousness and how to recreate them artificially will have to wait until the next book in this series due to the complexity and number of functions. Speaking of functions and the cortex is a little daunting at first pass; a popular way of dividing the cortex is with a map, Broadmann's areas, probably the most popular one contains some 52 areas, each one with a slightly different function, another consideration is the cortex structure itself, a series of layers with varied neuronal densities, connections and computations, tying this all together is the local and distant connections (the white matter) that creates local and distant networks.

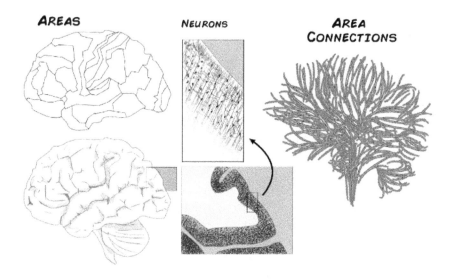

AREAS **NEURONS** **AREA CONNECTIONS**

As you might expect, disease or injury affecting the cortex results in either a specific deficit depending on the area and function affected, or a general one like with Alzheimers causing dementia, to give you an idea of how specific certain areas are, damage involving Broadmann's area 40 will create difficulty in understanding written and spoken language, but you would still be able to speak normally, Damage involving area 12 on the other hand would play out as disinhibited behavior, all those rules that society and common sense impose might still be present somewhere in your brain, but you would unfortunately lack the capacity to control your impulses resulting in cursing, awkward social behavior and other related effects.

***

Before leaving this overview of the Brains anatomy and function I would like to cover a couple of extra features that usually come up:

Gyri & Sulci

To account for a limited surface (the skull) the cortex is compressed, folded or crinkled into mountains (gyri) and valleys (sulci) much as if you were stuffing a large dinner napkin into a 3 dimensional object, the cortex itself (the layer of neurons) is of about the same size as the dinner napkin or about 1.3 square feet (0.12 m2) in size unfolded and about 2mm in thickness.

These folds and ridges develop both functional and anatomically as the brain matures at around the 5 month mark in infants. They vary from person to person although a few are constant, in general more surface area means more functional and cognitive capabilities vs a flat or smooth surface like that found in older animals (evolutionarily speaking), amongst humans though, there is no clear correlation in between brain size or number of ridges and cognitive abilities like intelligence.

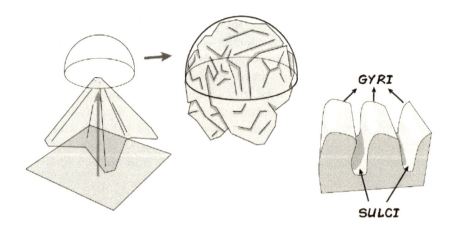

GYRI

SULCI

Cerebral Hemispheres and the Corpus Callosum.

One of the many quirks of the brain is that it is divided into 2 halves, the structures mentioned can be divided into almost symmetrical parts, most notably the cerebrum, which can be separated into two cerebral hemispheres, this division is believed to originate from the nature of many of our sensing apparatus and biology and how they have interacted with the environment trough evolution; for instance being capable of moving forward, an organism would benefit from left/right differentiation in sensing organs and processing.

Bilateral symmetry is observed across many species and can be considered one of a few routes that evolution took for the development of multicellular organisms, we could as easily have ended with radial symmetry or some other combination, the human body has a host of asymmetrical organs, so it is not a fully bilateral arrangement to start with, but there's a certain compromise of structures that fall into one or the other side.

The brain's hemispheres are connected by the corpus callosum, a thick band of axons that bounce back information from one hemisphere to the other, there are also other central areas where both hemispheres are connected called commissures. The notion that both hemispheres posses different functions has been ingrained in popular culture, the right side is creative, the left is analytic, 2 brains, maybe even 2 or more personas.

There is little evidence that this is the case, although there is functional differentiation, depending on the cortical area, the left and right hemispheres might just be processing stimuli from one or the other side of the body, in other areas though the difference is more nuanced, language for instance is left lateralized in most individuals, left and right areas are dominant in certain cognitive functions, and they might play a key role in certain aspects of consciousness like inner speech and self awareness.

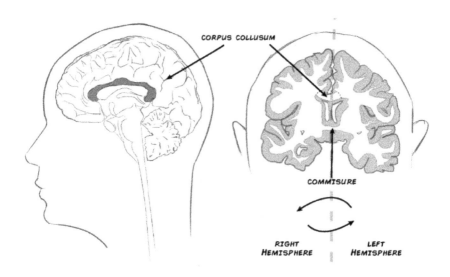

All these areas give us an important first functional division with informational pathways we can neatly summarize:

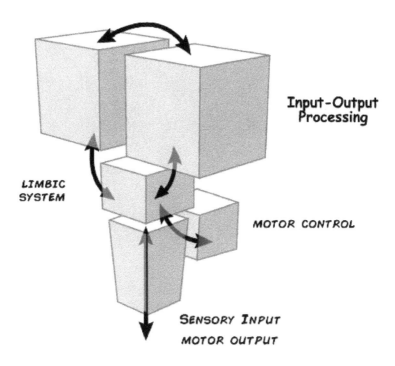

Input-Output Processing

LIMBIC SYSTEM

MOTOR CONTROL

SENSORY INPUT

MOTOR OUTPUT

A key consideration in examining brain structures and functions revolves around the integrative nature of them, but what do we mean by that ? The onion analogy comes to mind, if you were to peel one, you would start with the outer layers and keep removing them as they decrease in size until finally you were left with nothing, the onion disappeared without you finding any core or distinctive element, what makes the onion is the layers, the integration of them; and so with the brain and consciousness it is thought that rather than a single area, it is the sum of connections and information going back an forth that generates consciousness and many other cognitive functions.

***

Neurons.

The next core finding in neuroscience is that a nervous system is mostly populated by cells we call neurons, neurons both biological and artificial can be understood as the founding blocks of circuits, networks, systems and behavior which in turn are the substrate of consciousness, and so it pays to look at them a little closer.

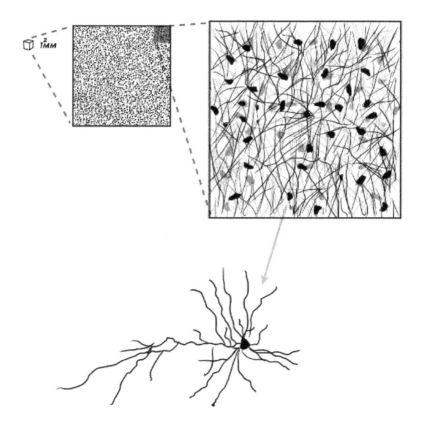

If you were to carve a 1mm cube out of the surface of the brain, chances are you would find about 100,000 neurons, slicing this cube and staining the neurons would give you a dotted square, and if you were to zoom into one of the corners, you would finally see some neurons in an interconnected mesh, isolating one of these black dots (the neuron body), you would end up with a single neuron as depicted.

There are 2 key attributes to neurons that other cells do not posses and by and large define them.. 1. They are focused in communicating with other neurons (*or signaling*) and 2. They can perform computations, a fancy phrase which means that depending on various circumstances they can change the way they communicate or not with other neurons depending on a number of factors, anatomically, they are differentiated by having 2 unique information pathways or processes which other cells like glia do not have.

Action Potentials

The communication or signaling in between neurons is accomplished by a mechanism called the action potential which employs both chemical and electrical elements.

A neuron signals other neurons through an electrical current generated via chemical interactions (*opening and closing of voltage* gated channels) that generate a change in the electrochemical gradient inside the neuron, this current in turn releases neurotransmitters which generate new chemical interactions in the target neuron and can propagate the electrical current.

A lot of extra complexity and nuance is involved, but for now it is convenient to think of the action potential as a binary (*1 or 0*) signal where 0 signifies a lack of current and 1 the presence of one; and the neuron as little machine whose job is to simply generate this type of signal.

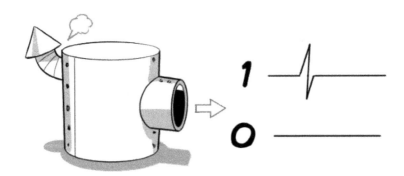

Basic Neuron anatomy

While neurons come in hundreds of varieties, the prototypical neuron consists of a cell body (*or soma*) , an input section (*dendrites*) and an output section (*axon or axons*) , in general action potentials are generated at the axon hillock and propagate through the axon where they connect with other neurons via their dendrites forming synapses.

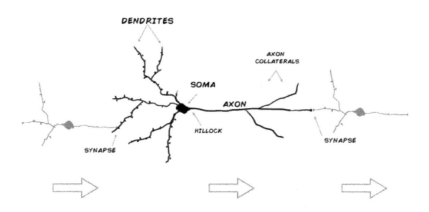

Basic neuron parts, actually 3 neurons are depicted here, one presynaptic, the one on the left, a target one, the one in the middle and a postsynaptic, the one on the right, action potentials go from left to right.

Once more it is convenient to think about this arrangement in abstract terms, this could simply be represented as 1s and 0s moving through our neuron machines:

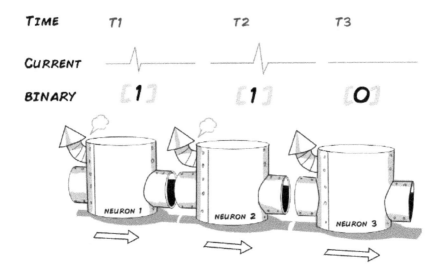

Note that the events depicted here are sequential in time, so the first one happens at Time 0 (or T1), the second one at Time 0+1 (or T2) and the 3rd one (in this case no action potential was generated) happens at Time 0+1+1 or T3, the actual current spike is also indicated in the middle.

It should be noted at this point that it is generally not well understood what level of detail is relevant for understanding consciousness, so a few other concepts that revolve around neurons might or might not be relevant or have a supporting role, here's a couple that could fall into that basket.

Neurotransmitters

As briefly summarized, the chemical/electrical nature of signaling in neurons is complex, one of the complexities lies in the way the electrical current propagates from neuron to neuron, it was thought for some time that the current just flowed from one neuron to the other directly at the synapses, much like a copper cable connected to another copper cable does, the electrons would flow (*or rather would be pushed or naturally drift*) freely. While this happens at some specialized connections in some animals (*like gap junctions*), the vast majority of neurons utilize neurotransmitters and chemical synapses.

A neurotransmitter is a chemical made inside the neuron in a packet (a synaptic vesicle) and sent across a tiny gap in between neurons at the synaptic cleft (the space between dendrite and axon), the neurotransmitters sent from one neuron travel a little distance and are received by the target neuron at specialized receptors, once inside the target neuron they can open ion channels which affect the neurons membrane potential, if the neurotransmitter is of the excitatory variety and there are enough of them, more channels will open and an electrical current will be generated, this electrical current in turn will release neurotransmitters at the connecting end of the neuron repeating the process and thus achieving communication in between neurons, this whole process usually happens in tenths of a second!

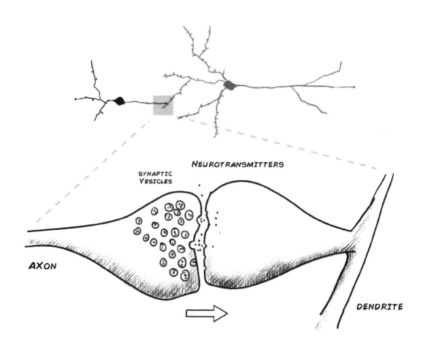

Detail of a synapse in between 2 neurons.

Resting potentials

Neurotransmitters allow for new and complex behavior, perhaps that's why they are employed by nature (*they add flexibility and new ways of dealing with the environment*), a sufficient quantity of neurotransmitters is now necessary to have an effect on the target neuron and produce a current, allowing varied computations with less expense; this resting potential is variable and affected by neurotransmitters, so the neuron can become less or more responsive; the next thing that neurotransmitters do is introduce variability. There are around 200+ types of different neurotransmitters, each one having a slightly different impact on the neuron or neurons they are sent to.

The effects though, can broadly be divided in 2, inhibitory and excitatory, and like their name implies they do just that, inhibitory neurotransmitters decrease the probability that the target neuron fires an action potential and excitatory ones increase the probability that the target neuron fires one. The 2 biggest neurotransmitters in the brain (around 90% of synapses) are from these 2 types: Glutamate (excitatory) and Gaba (Inhibitory). While there are neurons that produce them both, most stick to one or the other type.

Analogies... Our neuron machine analog now gets somehow more complex, the 1s and 0s now have an extra bit of information (are they excitatory or inhibitory ?) there is also now a threshold tied to the individual neuron or factory which symbolizes the minimum amount of neurotransmitters needed to effect change :

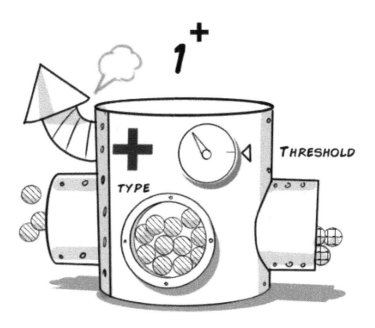

In our neuron machine, there is now a threshold, (resting potential), when enough neurotransmitters arrive to this threshold, the neuron releases it's own neurotransmitters to the next neuron, this threshold can be modified up or down by other neurotransmitters, additionally the neuron gets a type: excitatory (1+) or inhibitory (1-). As noted this is an analogy of a simple neuron, there are hundreds of neuron types and neurotransmitters.

***

You could be thinking that this complexity has little to do with consciousness, we will revisit and refine most of these concepts as needed, but to give you an idea as to how they relate to our main subject, take for instance gaba (*GABAA*), this inhibitory neurotransmitter is the main target of many anesthetics (*mentioned in the Anesthesia section*), increasing or promoting it's effect on neurons causes loss of medical consciousness, so we need to understand it's role if we are to understand consciousness.

While the biggest contribution of the discovery and research of neuro-transmitters is undoubtedly the pharmacology side which has developed a whole new range of medical treatments and drugs, for our focus though, the key finding is the added complexity which allows for computations, neural networks, cycles and systems to arise which all play a mayor role in consciousness both biological and perhaps artificial...but we are getting ahead of ourselves.

Let's finish with our summary of key findings from neuroscience; the following findings derive from the aforementioned and are of particular interest for consciousness since they form the plane onto which it exists.

***

Computations

You might be familiar with the term computations as it refers to calculations (both terms are somehow analogous) , which are loosely defined as transforming one or more inputs into one or more results with a variable change, adding or multiplying 2 numbers for instance is a calculation, you can be said to compute the result of this operation. There is an abstract side to computations which the field of Mathematics studies, but they become meaningful only when they are attached to something real like adding 2 apples or dividing a pie in between people.

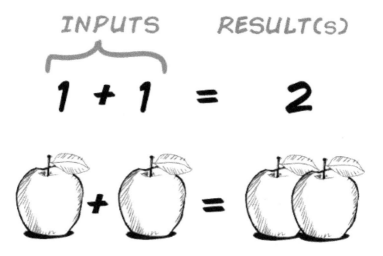

Neural computations broadly speaking refer to the transformations that neurons do to their inputs, the inputs in this case are from the environment through sensory neurons as well as internal inputs from one or more neurons or neuron assemblies, calculations are performed via multiple operations using a mix of connections, neuron types and temporal aspects, and can get quite complex; a common computation seems to be addition. If 2 or more presynaptic neurons connect to a third postsynaptic one with the right threshold, and they fire at roughly the same time, the third one will fire, in essence performing summation or addition:

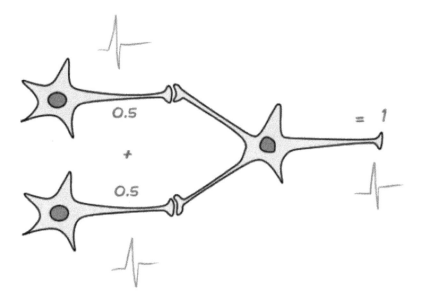

This simple neuronal circuit has been proposed as the basis for feature detection in the visual cortex, and might be widely employed elsewhere in the nervous system.

Things start getting more interesting when you add different types of neurons into the mix. Adding an inhibitory neuron to excitatory neurons for instance allows the neuronal circuit to put on the brakes on demand or in mathematical terms computing subtraction:

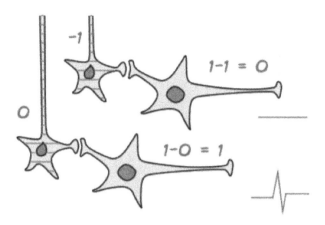

In this neural circuit, 2 descending inhibitory neurons synapse with 2 excitatory neurons, depending on which inhibitory neuron is active, the excitatory neuron is allowed or not to fire, this type of circuits have been predominantly observed in motor and muscle control structures, think about moving your finger or leg up and down, in the up position the down group of neurons is inhibited and vice versa.

Due to the flexibility imbued by neurotransmitters, connecting circuits and neuron assemblies (perhaps even whole networks or systems) can be turned on, off or modulated, in effect computing something complex (adding 2 numbers in your mind for instance), think of traffic lights allowing cars to move to a certain district, something we do when holding 2 possible answers in our head and allowing the correct one to go forth when we are convinced it's the right one, this would require additional circuits, but the switching aspect would be present in one or multiple places.

It is remarkable that the basic building blocks of our minds are simple in their nature and few in number, it is also sobering to realize that they can and are being combined in thousands of small and not so small circuits we barley understand or have begun defining, thankfully, it should be enough for now to know that they exist along with their basic operation, for we are still looking for insights and not necessarily detail, I'll leave this topic for now with one last circuit, in this case a logic gate (2-input Logic OR Gate) constructed with nothing more than the previously mentioned neurons.

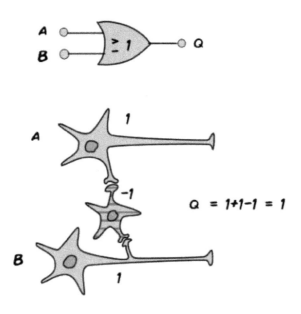

$$Q = 1+1-1 = 1$$

Logic Gates are the foundation of computer chips along with programming languages, in this microcircuit, either the A OR B neuron will fire, in the illustration, both A and B are firing, but since B connects to an inhibitory neuron that turns off A, only B ends up affecting downstream targets, the actual computation is Q, but you can construct a truth table for other cases.

***

N e t w o r k s ,   n e u r a l   n e t w o r k s .

"A country, a city, a neighborhood, a house and it's people".

Another important discovery and concept in Neuroscience is that of neural networks, which we'll overview without getting into specific networks for now.

A neural network is composed of a number of neurons connected in a specific way doing one or more specific functions or computations, we haven't yet discovered the specifics of most of these networks, what we have is a blurry image or general idea of where these networks are formed along with some functions they seem to support, this data usually comes in the form of healthy patients and brain imaging scans of them performing certain tasks, the resolution or actually the lack of detailed resolution has been an issue; historical though, patients which have unfortunately lost brain tissue due to misfortune or disease have also been invaluable sources of data via the correlation of affected areas and symptoms, a third and important source of insight into brain networks has been neuroanatomy, here the brain and brain tissue is examined and roughly divided into connections (synapses), computing units (neurons) and projections (axons and dendrites, although I like to use the word cabling), a daunting task due mostly to the size and number of the individual components (trillions, billions and microscopical), in short we don't have precise maps but rather a general idea of connections and the fact that there are regions across the brain that communicate with other regions and that this is an important part of the brains function, consider for instance the amount of real estate devoted to axons (white matter) vs neurons (grey matter) :

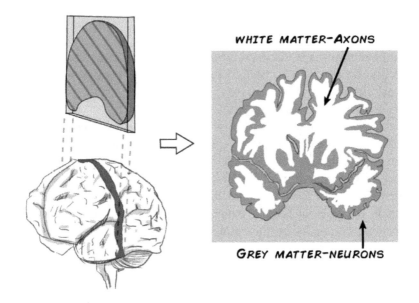

It also helps to think of this arrangement as axons representing cables and neurons smaller circuits affecting change somewhere else, much in the same way you toggle the switch in your living room and a light in your ceiling gets affected.

Additionally, we know that the predominant mode of operation in the brain is parallel, and both dispersed and localized.

The city analogy is a good place to start, there are people living in houses going about their daily business, neurons processing inputs and clustering in small and medium circuits, then there are neighborhoods or bigger systems of neurons and circuits devoted to more specialized functions; such neighborhoods can talk and join other boroughs to come up with bigger or more complex functions and finally all these neighborhoods or networks work together to form a city or town which from the outside is known to operate as a single entity producing a couple of important things, in the case of the brain all this activity helps the organism (or country in the analogy) survive and reproduce via a number of cognitive functions.

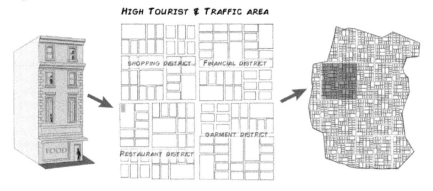

Communication in this analogy is performed by folks and their interactions within a building or neighborhood (locally) and through streets and highways (distant).

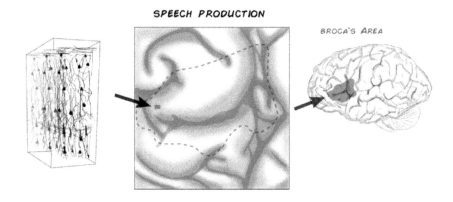

Speech is a complex cognitive function, Broca's area is but one of a number of areas involved, but it is thought to control speech production, but not cognition or vocabulary, so it communicates with other areas to produce language.

Another aspect; if we were to zoom into a couple of these neighborhoods at any one moment, we would probably find them busy doing their specific function, so neural networks are understood to operate in parallel, which is a good thing since a fire in one of them wouldn't necessarily shut down the whole city or country, a valid question then would be how are these areas synchronized?, we still don't know, but I believe synchronization is once more too broad a concept, certain areas could be synchronized based on sensory stimuli (bottom up), attention (top down), be autonomous via cycles, or a combination of these and other schemes changing over time; this brings us to the next key finding in neuroscience...

***

Cycles.

The sum of the electrical activity in the brain can be measured; and while our resolution is not all that great, it can be broadly divided into specific frequencies, amplitudes and cycles we call brain waves or neural oscillations:

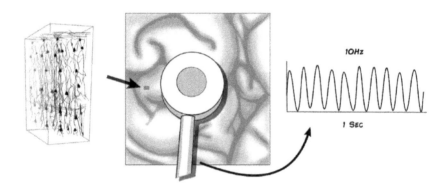

In practice, EEG measurements are taken across various regions and divided by sectors, one electrode like the one pictured can measure the underlying activity of millions of neurons firing action potentials periodically.

Brain waves are reveling in that they follow specific patterns of repeating activity, hence the cycle part, further they are tied up to specific structures or neural networks and resulting functions, so if x cycle appears when a certain function is performed and a set of brain areas are observed to be active through electrical measurements, a structured blueprint of the inner mechanics then can be inferred, and while this pales in resolution with other imaging techniques, it makes up for that with temporal resolution, which is of interest here.

Beyond this diagnostic function, the cyclic nature of the brains activity provides us with a partial answer to some of the trickier questions revolving consciousness, or at least one that I've always wondered about, what is the underlying mechanism for the permanence of consciousness ?

Have you ever wondered about the seemingly always on nature of consciousness?, that is you are always experiencing something even when there is not much to experience, say if you were locked in a white room for hours and hours with nothing to do, you would be aware of the white walls, maybe you would ignore them after a while, and then you would start thinking about something to pass the time, maybe you will get hungry eventually, but by and large you will always be experiencing something, one of the hardest things to do is think or experience nothing, why is that ?

In as few words as possible : *autonomous cycles*, the slightly longer and possible explanation is based on our previous tour of neuroscience findings: groups of neurons in your brain (certain neural networks) are periodically firing action potentials which are responsible for listening to the outside world or generating inner content (in both cases via neuronal computations), the firing happens in a cyclic manner, and while we are not quite sure of the details, a good candidate for this autonomous cycling is baseline release of neurotransmitters inside certain neurons, this neurons serve as pacemaker neurons and the subsequent propagation of action potentials in certain neuron groups coupled with autonomous synchronization due to the propagation of said action potentials.

The most surprising thing about this arrangement, is that certain populations of neurons seem to be periodically active all the time, so their corresponding cognitive functions are also active; but rather than having an always on nature, I would characterize them as being tuned down and expectant to further stimuli.

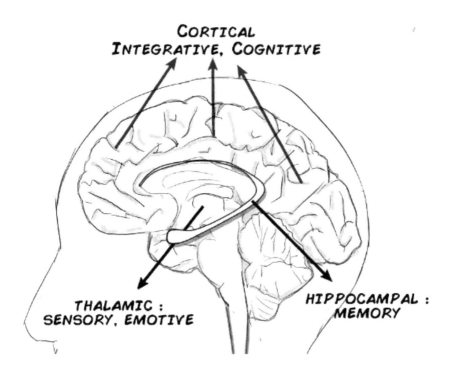

CORTICAL
INTEGRATIVE, COGNITIVE

THALAMIC :
SENSORY, EMOTIVE

HIPPOCAMPAL :
MEMORY

Primary brain regions and their corresponding functions where pacemaker neurons and autonomous cycles have been identified.

The integration of certain periodically active areas could be a good candidate for the substrate of consciousness; if you must stop this process, you can inhibit communication via chemicals like we reviewed in the anesthesia section or by restricting blood flow, which would unfortunately kill the neurons which then wouldn't be able to periodically secrete neurotransmitters, generate action potentials ,propagate information and would also be irreversible if it persisted for more than a few seconds. (*this happens in strokes and death*). But in the reversible case of anesthesia and temporary impaired consciousness states, the system of cycles and brain waves goes back to a predetermined state and set of rhythms. Exceptions do happen due to disease where one or more areas fail to regain synchronicity or suffer periodic irregularities like epilepsy and Parkinson's disease.

Another key finding involving cycles and electrical measurements is that of the periodic and regular nature of baseline neural oscillations against the mostly transient and seemingly chaotic nature when stimuli are present :

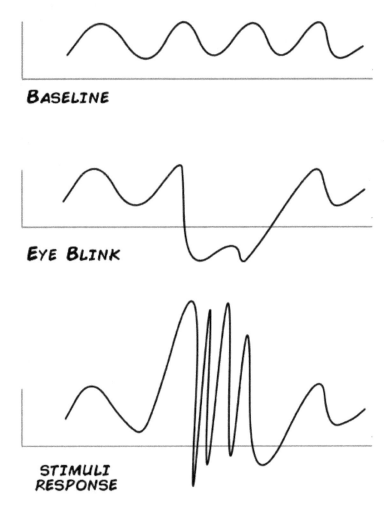

BASELINE

EYE BLINK

STIMULI RESPONSE

Generalized response to motor movements and stimuli from an EEG & Evoked Potentials.

Rather than the outside world bringing in some sort of order to a chaotic brain, it is believed to be the other way around; stimuli both external and internal present a chaotic signature that disrupts a stable baseline network rhythm, presumably to introduce information.

Synchronicity and Integration

So we have populations of neurons across the brain firing periodically, processing stimuli or at least waiting for them to be present and processed, note that other functions like memory consolidation might also be utilizing this baseline activity regardless of stimuli presence, the next consideration would be the integrative aspects of these autonomous neural cycles and their synchronization.

I would venture 2 basic ways in which neural networks can be synchronized, one locally through the periodic generation of action potentials and their immediate connections:

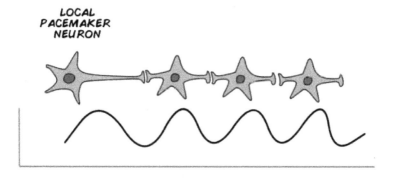

And second, long distance activation or coupling of a local neural networks via long distance synapsing of another local neuron group or network, which could also support the integration of information needed for consciousness:

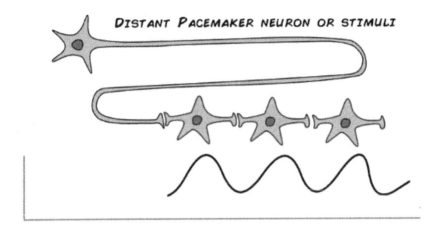

DISTANT PACEMAKER NEURON OR STIMULI

As we go about our days, a combination of both is probably the norm as we encounter and process stimuli or not at different levels of activity involving different brain areas.

Another clue to the integrative nature of consciousness comes from EEG recordings performed during anesthesia, as the dose of anesthetic increases, neural oscillations first decrease in frequency with deeper amplitude and at higher doses exhibit high intensity activity (or spindles) not unlike those found in certain sleep cycles, this finding could support the local/distant synchronicity mechanism, as communication wanes in between distant neuron populations isolated neural networks gradually loose the coupling and rhythm displayed in a bigger network and settle into a local one which is deeper, slower and eventually chaotic due to the lack of distant connections to modulate it, a high enough dose tends to all together extinguish oscillations.

ANESTHESIA

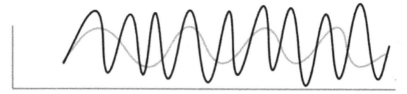

DEEP ANESTHESIA

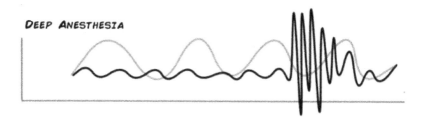

A change of areas can also be observed and as noted these are not precise measurements but rather rough indications of the underlying neuronal activity.

***

The following brief sections   build upon and expand our already established knowledge of neuroscience findings, once more they are not meant as detailed explanations but rather slightly more complex puzzle pieces...

Sleep.

Sleep is quite interesting as it relates to the study of consciousness; it falls into an altered or diminished state yet it is perfectly normal, even vital. It's quite common to think that sleep is a period of inactivity, both physical and mental, and while metabolic energy consumption does decrease, we believe it is not the only reason we sleep, restorative and homeostatic functions being the currently accepted primary reason, lack of sleep at its limits compromises our immunity systems and cognitive functions, so in this sense our bodies are actively healing and maintaining us during rest, additionally, the brain is quite active during sleep, even more so than during our waking ours.

Of particular interest to us, sleep presents (along with anesthesia) an instance where consciousness gets interrupted for a period of time and after a period of hours or minutes it resumes seemingly unaffected, it is not like anesthesia in that instead of a black bar that is placed during the 8 hours or so you might be sleeping, there are periods of deep sleep, light sleep and dreams, and as we will see, once sleep ends you are not the same person you were before, the neural mechanisms by which this happens every night or nap and the informational correlation is our focus here.

An initial consideration is that sleep comes in stages that can be summarized into **REM** and non-REM (where **REM** stands for Rapid Eye Movement, non-REM is also called Slow Wave Sleep), although there is a wide variety of behavior and additional intermediate stages, we can summarize them in EEG recording terms: deviations from baseline wakefulness by periods of mayor amplitude and minor frequency, minor amplitudes and high activity periods called spindles we already mentioned in passing; additionally there is a quality or degree of consciousness as it relates to being or not aware to stimuli and by how much, we'll dig deeper in a second, but during slow wave sleep you are barely responsive and in **REM** sleep you are fully unresponsive to stimuli.

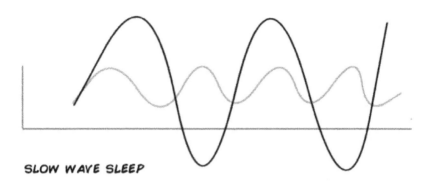

SLOW WAVE SLEEP

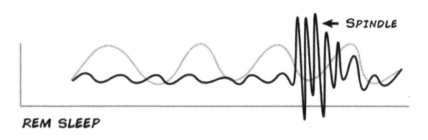

← SPINDLE

REM SLEEP

The mechanics of sleep seem to be inline with those of anesthesia which affect the GABA neurotransmitter, such mechanism is though to happen at sleeps onset and outset promoted by circadian rhythms or external stimuli via the limbic system. The result as you fall asleep is a release of inhibitory neurotransmitters that affect the integration of information but unlike anesthesia, also kickstarts a cycle mediated by additional neurotransmitters that result in sleep stages: acetylcholine mediates REM sleep in the cortex, Norepinephrine and Serotonin mediate slow wave sleep and the change of stages from REM to non-REM and vice versa.

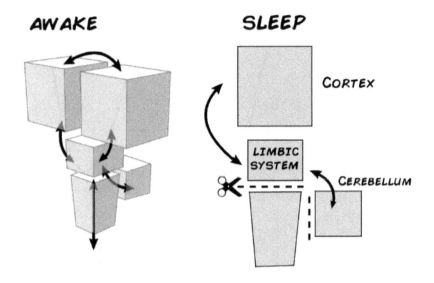

So at first sight sleep interrupts the information loop in between the cortex and the brain stem and cerebellum mediated by the limbic system and resulting in decreasing awareness of external and internal stimuli, this translates into you gradually loosing consciousness and the start of sleep stages involving the limbic system and cortex; another clue that points to integration as the main generator of consciousness and those areas as prime related candidates for generating it.

But there's more, if all the body and brain needed was a period of rest and regeneration, there would probably not be a need for an REM stage, but just a slow-wave period (tellingly, *older animals in the evolutionary tree like reptiles seem to lack REM sleep*). REM is peculiar in that the cortex seems to be at an extreme state of momentary activity, which paradoxically is higher than when we are awake, in contrast with this activity, muscle paralysis is at its highest and response to external stimuli is at its lowest, what could be happening here ?

The current accepted (and a little humbling) theory is that the REM stage is an evolution of tonic immobility. Tonic Immobility or Thanatosis is commonly observed in animals when they play dead as a response to predators, since predators usually prefer live pray, but what would grant such extreme and risky state ?

An opossum playing possum, an involuntary response triggered by fear where the opossum experiences paralysis and secrets a foul smelling odor, it seems to remain conscious but unable to move, a mostly successful evolutionary strategy for dissuading predators from eating it.

Tying this complex case is the informational component of sleep supported by the REM stage, as usual it is helpful to see what happens when REM and only the REM component is removed, in such experiments what ends up happening is an impaired cognitive state and a lack of memory formation or consolidation not unlike what happens after sleep depravation, the details are not all that well understood and we have yet to review memory and emotions, for now I would just summarize the REM stage as an informational replay of the events of the day along with a rebalance of the cognitive informational load in neural network which enables plasticity (i.e. long term memory consolidation) and a return to baseline cognitive behavior.

And Dreams ?

We don't precisely know why we dream, but based on the informational component and the integrative nature of consciousness we just
overviewed, we can venture that dreams are the result of the disconnect
of the brain from the environment combined with the replay of relevant
information acquired recently,(*during the past hours, day or days*)   there is
also an emotional component which segues nicely into our next section,
but for now let's recap and hopefully clarify by following a group of
neurons during sleep, as a reminder and self serving insurance, a lot of
this is theoretical and might be wrong in the detail:

When awake and using a certain neural network which supports a
cognitive function, neurons in that complex periodically get affected by
an influx of action potentials which taxes in some way it's performance,
the problem for that network is twofold: 1) it needs to be ready for the
next period of incoming information, and 2) it needs to perform better
based on todays interactions; during slow wave sleep the network gets
synced at a lower rate which allows it to replenish neurotransmitters and
be ready for the next day or period, the second part is taken care of by
replaying those networks and connections that were active during the
day, something that promotes the strength of those networks, on a macro
level, networks and functions that would intervene with these restorative
functions need to be turned off and on as needed.

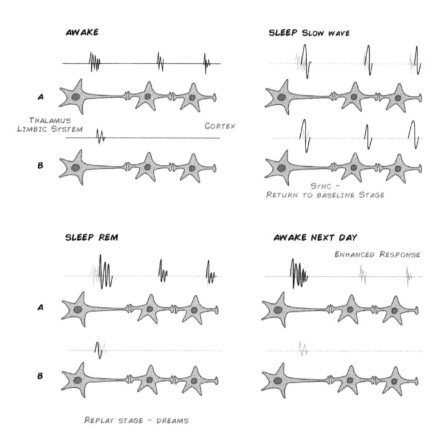

Proposed theory and comparison of 2 neural populations through the wake/sleep/ wake cycle, notice that network A replays information during REM sleep and presents a higher response the next day (in experiments with animals this can take days to weeks), network B though doesn't have the same REM replay and enhanced response, both return to a baseline state via the slow wave stage.

***

Emotions and Memory.

The limbic system plays a mayor role in at least 2 more relevant systems that might be of concern for consciousness: emotions and memory.

There is a lot of disagreements about the specifics and both subjects are vast, so once more this is an attempt to summarize very complex structures and processes into a few core concepts and ideas, let's start with emotions…

We can begin from the sensible agreement that we humans posses emotions, yet we somehow disagree on what precisely constitutes an emotion, we can further reasonably expect to categorize emotions into positive (trust, *serenity, joy*), negative (*fear, anger, sadness*) and somewhere in between or having extra qualities (amazement, anticipation, boredom) and perhaps even that they seem to be out of our direct or conscious control; some of us get very emotional about certain things, while others don't and there are a few we all seem to agree, like an empathic response to a genuine smile.

GENUINE SMILE   FEAR

Emotions are usually identified with facial expressions, a mostly involuntary outer display of our emotional state, an important and adaptive feature due to our social nature.

The first problem with emotions is that they are notoriously hard to define in narrow terms and the definitions we already have are fragile things that crack upon the pressure of closer inspection, this difficulty arises due to the variable nature of what affects us in the particular and the variety of biological responses emotions can represent; take for instance fear, if measured by it's biological or physiological responses we can observe increased heart rate, sweaty palms and increased alertness, the fear response puts us in what is called a flight or fight ready state, what could be so dangerous out there for the organism to experience this response ? In modern times for us humans it is nothing more than a school exam, we are ready to fight the paper in front of us or run away, maybe screaming; none of these things will helps us pass the exam and good luck defining that response in sensible terms, but we must.

Division and classification is also problematic, some researchers have tried to narrow down the types of emotions we posses, fear is a different emotion than say disgust, fear puts us in an alerted state while disgust marks the source as something to avoid, but we can easily prove that these emotions are not definitive since we can combine fear and disgust into a new emotion, like the emotion we experience when encountering insects, we are both scared and repulsed, shouldn't this then be a new type of emotion ? Fear itself can also be subdivided into subcomponents; some might get sweaty palms just by watching a specific event like someone free climbing a building, but not necessarily be scared or more alert, so we haven't quite narrowed specific responses to emotional states, we need to take a step back and dig deeper or plainly define emotions as anything that evokes a response...let's dig deeper.

Why have emotions in the first place ?

The story on how we ended up with these complex things called emotions requires us to revisit the brain as a progressively constructed

76

house, emotions might make more sense when viewed as part of a system focused on survival and reproduction which in turn inhabits a changing and complex environment.

Viewed under this light, emotions first provided the functionality of allowing the organism to pass on (via random processes or genes) specific adaptive behavior and responses that would be conducive to the survival and reproduction of the organism and its offspring, later additions incorporated complex processing of stimuli that could be attached to these responses (mainly learned and social) , let us examine how this might have played out with the fear response to try and clarify this point.

It's a dangerous environment that doesn't give many second chances, there is no shortage of things that could kill and organism. Learning about the dangers out there through trial and error it could get devoured the first time it encountered a predator or perish the first time it reached a cliff, this type of encounters and their outcomes need to be somehow deducted and avoided beforehand, so what evolution seems to have come up with is a generalized response based on learned close calls passed on to the offspring, or even random mutations if you subscribe to strict natural selection; an organism that scurries away from a big thing with fangs can survive and reproduce, a flight or fight response to the same stimuli improves the odds of scurrying away on time, and a fear response that can be passed down then improves the odds of survival for the whole lineage.

The reward system constitutes a subjective opposite to fear within the positive emotions category, the organism actively seeks something to get a reward and when this behavior and response gets incorporated into the organism and passed down to further generations, the odds of survival are better.

This is a good place to introduce emotion related neurotransmitters which serve as more convenient replacements to hardwiring behaviors and responses, they also seem to serve as generalized evolutive tools for dealing with multiple stimuli and responses within a limited biological real estate, Dopamine for instance is believed to increase the saliency or importance of a stimuli as it relates to reward, in the fear response there are a number of neurotransmitters each with a different effect, nor-epinephrine for instance increases arousal and alertness, I believe if one were to look for primordial emotions each neurotransmitter that affects our baseline cognitive state would be a good place to start.

78

The latest addition to our emotional system is the higher processing of stimuli, this processing involves associations with stimuli that the organism now learns during its lifetime and generates a 2 way interplay in between instinctual emotions (those we are born with or are predisposed to) and those we learn during our lifetimes, this dramatically expands the usefulness of emotions since we can attach them to novel stimuli, if we see 2 medium sized things with fangs devouring our relative, we can now add them to our fear response, this is an elegant solution that unfortunately doesn't work 100% of the time, we can fool the reward system by ingesting neurotransmitters (you might know them simply as drugs), attach an emotion to the wrong stimuli (like money) or have a useless response to something we seem to have attached an emotion by association or other cognitive process (like the school exam).

Even under this short examination we can get important insights: consciousness and our higher cognitive or rational self are mostly relegated to the passenger side while emotions influence and guide our actions, we are still capable of unemotional actions, but   it is only when our intelligence and emotions are in agreement, or at least emotions not interfering, that we perceive intelligence and reason to have the upper hand, trying to overcome our emotions is hard due to their deep-seated nature both literally and figuratively, to get the full picture of how emotions behave in this manner would need a review of Memory system in the brain which we will sample now.

***

Memory

Memory along with consciousness has always been a particular interest of mine, by necessity and from experience we need to once more summarize and focus, we could start from the consideration that memory is not an unitary concept, but rather a set of related processes we usually bunch into the term memory, we could then talk about each one of this processes, but I think its best to leave the specifics for a later section and book, as with anything perhaps it is best to start from a very basic and practical definition since we are still talking about findings and hopefully wander up hill from there...

The world a conscious organism inhabits is composed of other elements that exist in a material and temporal space, memory can be understood as extracting representations of environmental and internal stimuli as well as the organisms own responses with the purpose of then carrying them along in time and space for the organisms use and benefit.

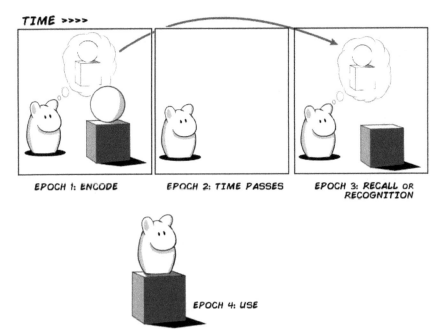

EPOCH 1: ENCODE   EPOCH 2: TIME PASSES   EPOCH 3: RECALL OR
                                                     RECOGNITION

EPOCH 4: USE

Simple view of memory processes: acquiring stimuli (encoding), letting time pass, recalling stimuli- note the imperfect nature of the recall and the prompt, the stimuli can also just be recognized, have I seen this before ? (yes/no) and finally using the memory in some way (hopefully useful).

Permanence of stimuli is then the domain of memory, in a gross manner memories can be divided by how long they stay with the organism, short-term, long term and by how accessible they are to consciousness, other divisions involve their content; like facts, behavior or what happened to the organism, there even is a memory type devoted to volatile information we can manipulate and discard, a sort of computational buffer we call working memory, here's a sampling of memory types:

DOMAIN ⟶

DURATION

SENSORY
(<= SECONDS)

ICONIC   ECHOIC   HAPTIC
(IMAGES)   (SOUND)   (TOUCH)

SHORT TERM
(SECONDS-MINUTES)

WORKING MEMORY
(MANIPULATION OF STIMULI)

LONG TERM
(DAYS - YEARS)

ACCESS

DECLARATIVE / EXPLICIT

(CONSCIOUS RECALL)

EPISODIC
(WHAT, WHEN, WHERE)

AUTOBIOGRAPHICAL
(EVENTS IN OWN LIFE)

SEMANTIC
(FACTS, ABSTRACT KNOWLEDGE, THIS IS THAT)

PROCEDURAL / IMPLICIT

(UNCONSCIOUSS)

PRIMING   MOTOR SKILLS

Notes: *This is probably an incomplete table, for starters there are other domains not included, short term and long term memories for instance can also have a domain element (visual, tactile, etc, etc). additionally some types can be combined multiplying the types, and what to say about individuals whose memory types are completely different to baseline subjects, visually impaired subject can use echolocation to navigate their surroundings and presumably can memorize this new type of content, and obviously the types we haven't discovered...*

How these stimuli are encoded and hold through time is nothing short of amazing considering we can retain memories for decades and the machinery that supports this function is composed of living cells.

The key finding here that can help summarize the neuroscience of memory at the macro level is that we don't store perfect copies of stimuli, but rather imperfect traces of the original experience; when we recall memories we are replaying the same networks that were active during the original experience, although sometimes we do a little curating and memories have a life of their own not consciously accessible due to the nature of live recurrent networks of neuron connections, their substrate.

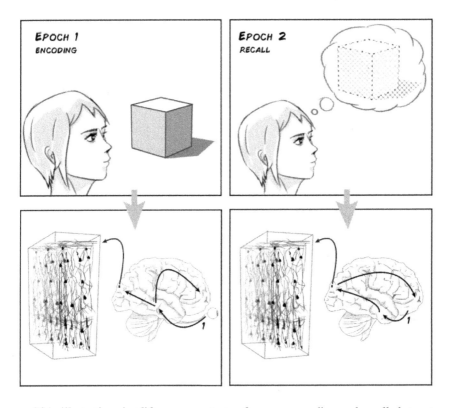

This illustration simplifies many aspects of memory encoding and recall, but note that upon recall there is a different order and networks employed than with encoding, bottom up where the stimuli starts from the environment and top down where the recall starts internally.

A second important insight (still at the macro level) is that there is an integrative nature not unlike that to consciousness where multiple brain areas serve the same function, in the case of memory, the limbic system and the cortex once more play mayor roles, the limbic system (specifically the hippocampus), initiates the process by marking relevant stimuli (internal or external) for memory consolidation, the cortex where these stimuli were originally experienced initially consolidates stimuli via stronger connections involving the limbic system, but after a period these networks can become more isolated, establishing long term memories that can also interact with other parts of the cortex, this is the foundation of complex concepts and associations we can later produce, once consolidated the hippocampus and other areas are still needed to access established memories, so while they might live in the cortex, the road to them sometimes lies elsewhere, mainly the hippocampus or associated cortical areas.

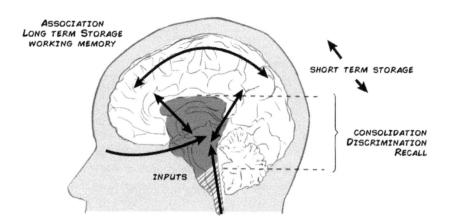

Like with the onion and consciousness, it seems that what we call memory involves the whole brain, and not a single area is responsible for every aspect, here we graphically summarize some types of memory, process and relevant areas.

At the micro level neuronal connections become stronger initially due to resting potential levels and neurotransmitter interactions, there are also specific transient states like working memory where specific neural networks are recruited, but in the long term new connections in between neurons seem to be created via axonal targeting and dendritic growth.

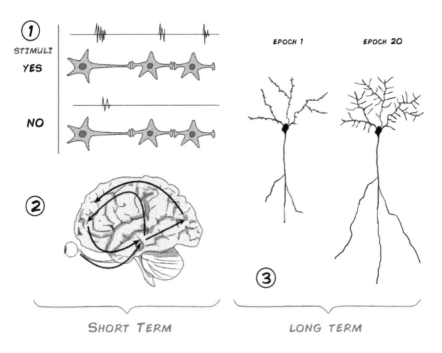

Overview of the proposed neural mechanism of memory (or plasticity) 1. Neurons that fire together stick together through reinforcement, 2. Populations of neurons firing in a cyclical manner can maintain stimuli in short term or working memory, 3. Long term memory strengthens connections and makes new ones through axonal & dendritic growth.

***

Memory, emotions and sleep.

Another relevant aspect for consciousness is the intersection of related functions and how they complement and work together, in this case, memory, emotions and sleep form part of a system devoted to storing relevant information in a periodic way, with or without the organisms conscious involvement or awareness, we'll use this insight for the next section involving the subconscious...

At any given moment we are being bombarded by thousands if not millions of stimuli and we discard most due to our limited sensory biological apparatus, out of those we can perceive, the question then becomes which ones are relevant to our survival and reproduction ?

Emotions seem to serve as markers for storing important memories, it should be noted that they are not the only way into memory, repetition or stimuli saliency can also provide this function and memory is widely distributed throughout the brain, anatomically, the limbic system location makes sense as a sort of gatekeeper that is constantly consulting innate and acquired emotional relevancy with the cortex and marks incoming content accordingly, additionally it directs attention towards relevant stimuli in essence reinforcing existing emotions with new relevant content.

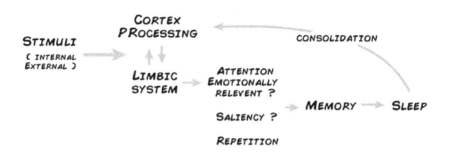

Simplified view of the emotional/memory/sleep process

If emotions are the gatekeeper of memories, sleep is the groundskeeper; sleep and neuronal rest seem to affect memory consolidation from the relevant content marked during the day and other timespans into medium and long term memories, such consolidation could be caused by an initial rebalancing of resting potentials in between neurons, which is based on the replay of the days events marked by emotions, this mechanism allows for an unlimited number of memories to be stored and ordered according to the organisms perceived value. The transition from medium to long term memories then can proceed via chemical signals that more firmly synaptically connect up these sensory networks; while neurons are more or less constant in number after a certain age, the connections (dendrites and axons) are not, the vast computational power and storage capacity of the brain seems to lie here.

Once consolidated into medium or long term memories, these stimuli are not cast in stone; without being revisited they can become harder to recollect, here the physical mechanism is a retraction of dendritic branches and axons, something similar happens in some memory and cognitive related diseases, but when the organism is healthy the now established memories are part of a live self-encoding and self-updating network that lies behind higher cognitive functions like imagination and creativity.

***

Subconsciousness.

A discussion about consciousness wouldn't be complete without taking into consideration the subconscious; rather than a loss of consciousness as already explored in the anesthesia section, when we talk about the subconscious or unconscious mind, what we are referring to is those processes that affect behavior but are not available to our conscious self, I know we haven't quite defined consciousness at this point, but we have enough knowledge to define the subconscious.

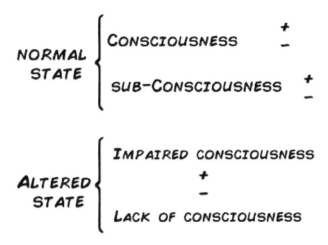

Subconsciousness is a normal biological state, it is yet unclear what happens with it during an altered state, here in both cases there are gradients or levels of consciousness (the +-)

Consider the previous sections and mechanisms on memory, emotions and sleep; when we are experiencing a stimulus we can be said to be focused or attending to it, attention then is a component of consciousness we'll have to later revisit, for now it's enough to note what attention is in the general sense, look at any object in your immediate vicinity, focus on it, that's attention. You can also attend to other stimuli, like sound, taste, touch etc, etc.

Stimuli that we attend to have a greater probability to be memorized and recalled, but we are also blissfully unaware of a number of things that bypass the limbic system gatekeeper and end up in our memories, additionally due to the emotional influence on what gets marked for memory and how important it is, we can end up with unwanted and unrelated memories of stimuli that just happened to occur at the time of a highly emotional event, PTSD and that once awful song (now awesome) that was playing during your first kiss or an emotional moment are common examples.

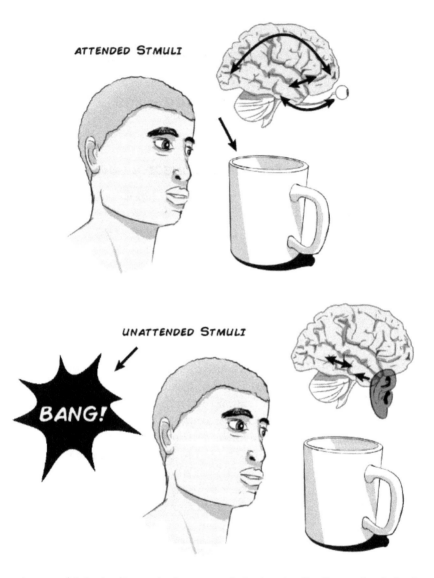

An unattended stimuli can also be generated via the stimuli saliency, that is by the nature of it being different in some particular way, most commonly by it's intensity, in either case the important distinction is that it bypasses higher processing from cortical areas.

A second unconscious mechanism is related to memory consolidation; as mentioned, memories once marked for storage go through a number of processes that change the connections in between the groups of neurons that processed the original stimuli, if during a day, two or more stimuli are coded at roughly the same weight or time, they might end up firing in an ordered progression at a later date, this is the basis of associations and they can happen without us being aware, look at an object around you, what is the first thing that object reminds you ?, the second and third ? Do you remember how and when you initially stored those objects along with the instructions that they will appear in that order when presented with the original one ? The answer for most of us is no, that is unless we co opt the system for our own self directed goals, something that is not achieved without considerable effort, just ask any student...

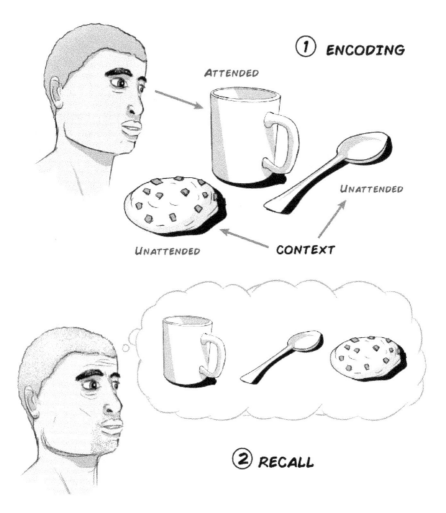

Those stimuli that are not consciously attended and make their way into memory can also be considered context and can be used to retrieve the original stimuli, present stimuli to get context, present context to get stimuli, in other ways they seem to have a two way relationship.

A 3rd related unconscious process takes us back to neural pacemakers, populations of neurons representing stimuli are periodically firing action potentials; said action potentials affect plasticity (*memory consolidation*) and connections in between similarly active populations, if you incorporate newer stimuli you now have a soup of old and new populations interacting and creating new combinations of representations, this is a proposed mechanism for creativity, which once more lies outside of our immediate attention. It should be noted that artists, and creative professionals are somehow aware of this process and are constantly trying to feed the creative side with new stimuli, professional designers for instance use mood boards, a collection of images related to the product's style, color, and other elements which the brain ends up connecting into newer creations.

Subconscious processes seem like a mistake or deviation from evolution, but a mutation only needs to be a net positive to the organism's survival, or at least not a net negative, there is also the matter of it preceding consciousness in the evolutionary tree, so in that sense it is consciousness the interloper that needs to justify it's utility and recent addition, once more these topics will have to wait for a more in depth discussion, for now it is sufficient to note that we posses both processes which are active in different measures depending on the individual and specific stimuli , a little disconcerting and anticlimactic, but then again if you were to describe a human to an alien, one of the distinctions would be that it is an organism capable of seemingly endless new behavior and also a capable of focused repetitive behavior, best of both worlds!

Is that it ?

Well yes and no, these are the basic ingredients if you will and there is still a lot of detail needed to make sense of consciousness, things like the specific brain waves and how they tie up to consciousness, specific brain areas and their cognitive or functional correlates and the daunting task of summarizing both small local circuits and global networks which can serve as a foundation to later try starting to reproduce them artificially... but as a brief overview of the elements of the problem I hope it serves. I would now like to change gears and briefly review the other side of our problem, Artificial Intelligence.

***

Artificial Intelligence

Artificial Intelligence or A.I. is a fairly recent (*around 1950's*) field of research and increasingly real world applications.

In general one can think about Artificial Intelligence as any process or computation we can apply to a problem that is somehow related or emulates human or biological intelligence, a narrower definition would be that of any artificial construct that perceives its environment and takes it into consideration for action which can then help it succeed in a task.

It is hard coming up with a satisfactory definition because well, we haven't quite come to an agreement as to what intelligence is, something we will discuss soon, other difficulties arise due to the multitude of domains that have used the term, let's have a brief look:

Culture.- (*Movies, Books, Video Games*) A.I.s are usually portrayed as presenting some human traits, although traditionally emotions have been left out to focus on the logical, calculating part; they are usually an antagonist or plot device, there's usually some mention of the Turing test and save for a precious few have very little connection to reality which is unfortunate since most people are familiar with this version.

Academia.- At the polar opposite of culture, academia has tradition-ally been the originator of research and prototypical A.I.s and while it has tried to formalize concepts; a clear standard or consensus has yet to be reached and maybe it will never be, instead what we have are very narrow definitions of theoretical and applied A.I.s, things like neural networks and search algorithms that are defined in mathematical or logical terms.

Industry.- Industry doesn't traditionally care too much about getting concepts and definitions right, but due to the economic incentives, whatever term is given to a particularly successful solution for a problem gets popularized, so currently (*late 2018*) machine learning and deep learning are buzz words and the term A.I. is used on products that use only very specific techniques or algorithms to do their function; marketing probably thought *A.i. Powered* sounded better than database search with custom algorithms, and so there's A.i. powered gadgets everywhere.

So we have a couple of basic and incomplete definitions and some extra usage, let's briefly overview a few of the more common A.I.s in use to get a feel for the current state of the A.i.

Rather than try yet one more time to come up with definitions, let's instead define a problem and try solving it with some A.I. techniques:

Our problem will simply be to move across a room from an initial position to the exit at the other end (*a newborn and many animals can do this*), we can always add complexity by adding some obstacles, but for now let's keep it simple:

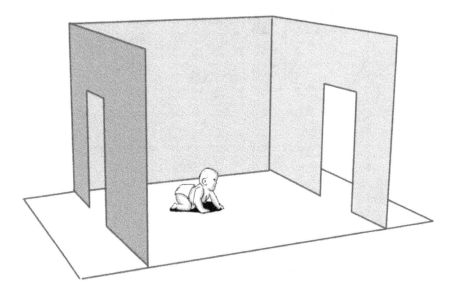

The first thing we would need to do is reconstruct our problem into a form suitable for a computer to solve, in reality we would just place our newborn at the initial position in a room and dangle something shiny at the exit; to make this particular problem suitable for an A.i., we can divide the room into a numbered grid, mark the initial and target (*or exit*) positions and provide some rules to the A.i. like giving it turns and allow it to move x amount of spaces per turn, mark the walls and obstacles as no go zones and specify a suitable result (*final position = exit position*).

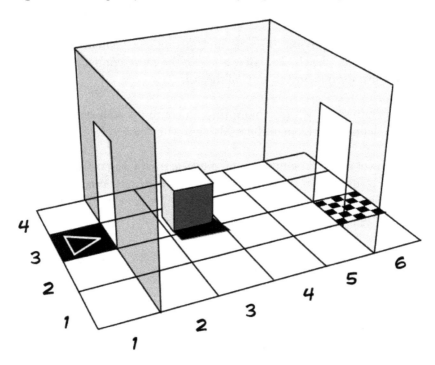

Perhaps one of the biggest drawbacks to this arrangement is that by necessity we are providing a proxy or second rate version of reality, we are also skipping specific implementations, but any computer language and novice programmer can recreate these basic examples.

Search, Logic & Algorithms:

A common solution (*and a good place to start*) is to employ some mathematical rule or algorithm to get us closer to the exit; we could for instance list all the possible spaces we could move to, compute the final position and compare that to our target or goal and then simply chose one of the resulting paths that gets us to the exit.

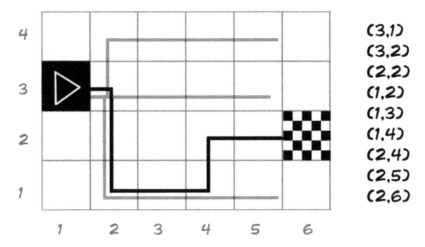

(3,1)
(3,2)
(2,2)
(1,2)
(1,3)
(1,4)
(2,4)
(2,5)
(2,6)

Here we present a few unsuccessful paths and one of many successful ones along with the coordinate readout, while you might think this is child's play or a simplistic example, this is the blueprint for trial and error that underpins many biological processes and behaviors, you might even be undergoing some version of it right now.

For now we are not interested in doing this efficiently, but if we were, we would add algorithms, statistical methods and logical elements to maximize our efforts, much of the current complexity and development of A.I.s is devoted to doing things in an efficient or automated way, machine learning is currently focused on that…

Machine learning:

Another approach is machine learning, here we are very loosely emulating how humans and animals learn and improve their actions towards achieving a certain goal, in our example we could start with a random path and measure it against our goal (arriving to the exit), then through a statistical algorithm and other techniques modify it so subsequent trials get closer. Machine learning can be supervised (we are guiding the learning through training) or unsupervised, we let our a.i.

figure out on it's own the learning and mapping of inputs (*positions on the board*) to outputs (has it arrived to the *exit or not*), it still needs to be programmed to do so though.

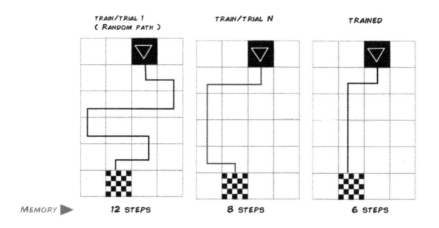

The memory or learning component in this simple case is represented by keeping track of how many steps it took to arrive to the exit, the goal then becomes finding the solution with the least amount of steps, but it could be anything else, finding food or a mate for instance.

Artificial Neural Networks:

Artificial Neural Networks (*or ANN*) as the name implies try to artificially recreate biological neurons and their connections to solve a problem, rather than an exact copy of their biological counterparts, ANNs emulate basic components and certain qualities like the relationships in between individual neuronal circuits and learning.

ANNs have become quite complex and employ a mix of statistical and biological insights, but if we cheat a little (*by removing obstacles and making the problem linear*) we can construct a simple one to solve our problem:

Our Neural Network will simply consist of 3 neurons, a sensory one , a processing one and a motor one, the sensory neuron receives an input of

1 if the tile ahead is empty or 0 if it is not, the middle neuron (or inter neuron) is in charge of deciding what to do, if the tile is empty, it will inform the motor neuron to advance one tile:

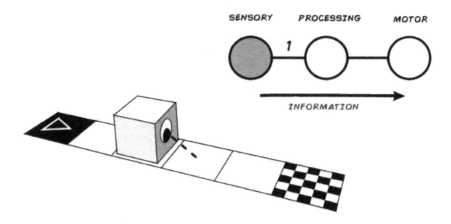

In case it's not clear, the sensory neuron is the big eye in front and the motor neuron could be some wheels underneath the Ai.

In order to detect the exit, we need to add another sensory neuron, this neuron will only fire if it perceives the exit, else it will not.

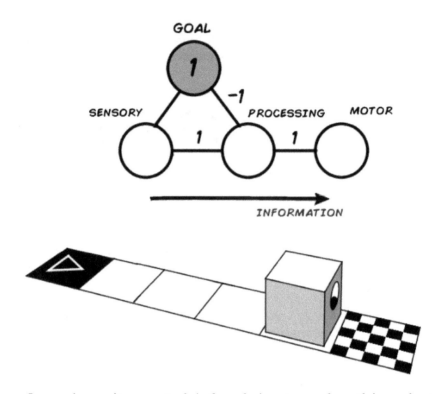

In general, our exit neuron stands in for goals, in nature, goals are their own beast and can be hardcoded or variable.

The inter neuron (middle neuron) then decides what to do based on a set of rules that loosely mimic inhibitory and excitatory neurotransmitters and neuronal circuits; we are signifying these by the lines in between neurons and the weights marked on them, we are also marking when a neuron fires with a greyed (just fired) or darkened (is firing) neuron in pseudo graph notation:

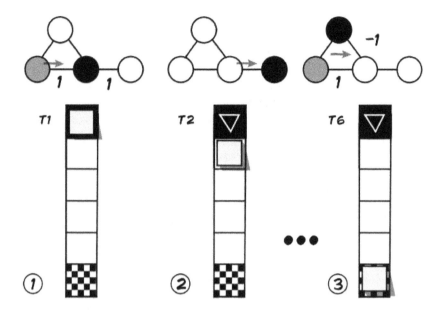

1. The sensory neuron fires (light grey) and in turn the processing neuron fires in black (indicated by the number 1 in both cases) 2. Movement is then achieved by the firing of the 3rd neuron in black. 3. Upon reaching the goal, the 4th neuron fires, note that its weight is negative and cancels the positive one from the first sensory neuron, thus stopping the A.i.s movement.

Also of note, our neural network is already trained, that is the weights in between the neurons are such that the behavior (*moving and stopping when the exit is found*) works. The process of arriving to these weights and behavior is called learning, so in this sense and use, **ANNs** are currently a subset of machine learning.

Pattern recognition:

Pattern recognition is another branch of A.i. that deals with recognizing if something is of a certain kind or not, this is a powerful tool for biological animals, is this animal going to eat me or can I eat it ?

Pattern recognition can be solved in a brute force way by having a database of patterns and then simply searching the database for the observed pattern, this unfortunately can be computationally expensive, yet it seems to be employed widely in nature.

Other ways of solving pattern recognition have emerged (*inspired by vision science*) and are currently   state of the art A.i.s, these techniques involve the use of statistical methods and/or neural networks (deep learning, convolutional neural networks) that have been designed to divide the original problem, extract features and predict if it matches a pattern or can be classified as something we are looking for.

For our problem of finding the exit and getting out of the room we can just use a simple database and search algorithm to classify what our a.i sees in front, if it is an empty tile, advance, if it is an obstacle go around it, if it is the exit stop and so on. While the problems solution is simple at first sight, in reality it is far more complex, consider for instance that the Ai will be looking at the room from its own point of view, and would need to extract features and derive meaning from them:

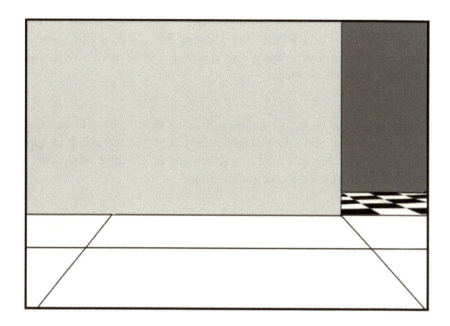

This short list will surely grow with time and is by no means exhaustive or an in depth look at any one A.i, but rather serves as a short introduction or review of common A.i.s.

***

Down the rabbit hole.

So we now have some basic concepts under our belt, these will help us while parsing more complex aspect of consciousness which in turn will help us ease into the artificial ones, think of these as slightly bigger puzzle pieces…

Intelligence and Consciousness

Intelligence is another one of those concepts we all seem to easily recognize, but yet is hard to pin down with a specific definition, non the less we will try to add to the ever growing list of definitions, here for instance a common dictionary one that twists itself into a deliciously redundant semantic pretzel:

"The ability to learn or understand or to deal with new or trying situations : reason; also : the skilled use of reason (2) : the ability to apply knowledge to manipulate one's environment or to think abstractly as measured by objective criteria (such as tests)"

I believe that a short, general & practical definition of intelligence can first be composed of a goal or purpose, an actor or actors and whatever actions that these actors do to successfully realize their goal, so a plant can be intelligent if it responds to its environment by signaling other plants or a fungus by releasing spores at the right time, they both have a purpose (to reproduce or survive) and their actions can be considered intelligent if they help them realize that goal.

This definition is broad enough to also encompass machine intelligence and human intelligence, although their goals are not the same, humans are bound to the biological goals of survival and reproduction, while machines are not and so their goals can be anything that one programs them to do (including survival and reproduction), so paradoxically a machine can be intelligent even if the goal is to destroy itself, the inventor or programmer of such machine could even be considered intelligent if he had a goal, perhaps to prove a point...

Since our language is our invention and we are a proud species, we have defined intelligence from a human point of view, so intelligence is closely related to our cognitive abilities, it is this set of cognitive abilities that we will explore and focus, not because they necessarily are the sole source of consciousness but because it will simply make our lives easier to differentiate one from the other when possible.

Cognitive Abilities:

Since we are talking about cognitive abilities, an overview is needed, let's imagine that a superior alien race has gotten ahold of a pair of humans and is auctioning them to the highest bidder for some intergalactic zoo or collector, so our entrepreneurial alien would present the humans in a stage and start listing the features: they can move, make noises, grow hair etc, etc. A tentacle would then raise from the audience and ask "But are they intelligent ?" and the alien will then briefly list our cognitive abilities trying to make a sale:

- These here humans posses memory, so they can remember events and facts, they even remember events and facts about themselves, they can also use their memory to learn new knowledge and later use those things in new ways.

- Humans can make decisions, that is they can consult their memory and use it for better results, so if you present them with 2 pieces of food, they will take the one they like the best or won't make them sick.

- Humans are capable of thoughts and ideas, inner representations of real and unreal things, they can also generalize representations and deal with the abstract, all by themselves with no extra tools or devices.

- Humans can also communicate with each other in meaningful ways, conveying meaning about themselves, others, their environment and knowledge, they even have a limited understanding of what other humans are thinking or experiencing.

- And above all, humans use their intellect to adapt to their environment through the use and creation of tools, their senses, motor skills and knowledge; both acquired and passed on to them by other humans and inherited traits.

This is of course not a complete list, but it will hopefully be enough for a record setting bid and for us to get a general idea about cognitive abilities, in short they can be considered a number of processes that occur in the brain/nervous system and subserve the organisms goals with

104

added nuance and complexities.A reflex for instance is not usually considered a cognitive ability, the division is somehow arbitrary but it helps to think of processes that are either conscious (self directed or involving awareness) recruit other cognitive abilities or are a result of computations and more basic responses.

Intelligence vs Consciousness

What relationship does Intelligence have with consciousness, are they perhaps the same ? On the surface consciousness could be considered part of intelligence, but if we look a little closer this notion falls apart, take for instance instincts and memorized responses like muscle memory, we are not aware of our responses in a conscious way, yet by many standards they are intelligent responses, on the other end there is consciousness as an act of experiencing, so if there is no problem to solve this type of consciousness is not very intelligent.

I propose a truce, or rather a Venn diagram where intelligence and consciousness coexist in the same plane and mingle occasionally:

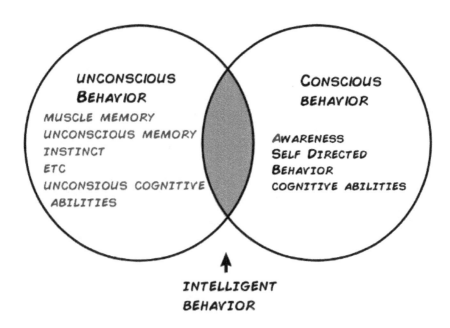

The size of the circles is variable, on one end we have unconscious behavior
that once was useful for our survival and now since our goals have changed does not,
on the other we have conscious behavior that can result in detrimental effect, its a
complex an changing relationship.

So the relationships is one where we can have conscious intelligent behavior, (we can communicate our plans of escaping an alien prison to a fellow human for instance), unconscious intelligent behavior (like instinctively spitting a toxic and bitter tasting alien cracker) or purely conscious (like noticing the passage of time).

***

The Hard problem of consciousness.

The Hard problem of consciousness asks a very related question to the nature and elements of consciousness we are exploring, why do we experience something when perceiving our environment and our thoughts, and more importantly why is the nature of such experience of the subjective kind. For instance, why do we feel pain, why do we perceive the color red and taste something as bitter or sweet ? And why are these experiences different from one another ? This hard to place concept has been given the name qualia and it is heavily debated.

I believe the hard problem is hard because it demands an easy answer to a complex process, it's also not entirely clear what qualia is. We can start by stating some facts and solving it partially by noting that each of the above sensations is particular, the sensory cells devoted to perceiving the color red, the ones devoted to pain (*or nociceptors*) and those for taste are each of a different kind:

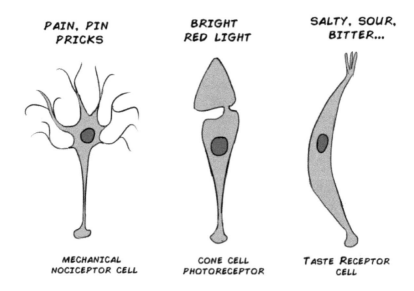

PAIN, PIN PRICKS

BRIGHT RED LIGHT

SALTY, SOUR, BITTER...

MECHANICAL NOCICEPTOR CELL

CONE CELL PHOTORECEPTOR

TASTE RECEPTOR CELL

So the easy answer is that they all feel different because they all are different in nature, it is only our concept of mind that brings them together, so qualia can then be defined as the integration of different stimuli into a perceived whole.

This point is worth exploring a bit more, remember from the evolution chapter that the vast majority of our mental machinery has a purpose, in the case of perceiving stimuli the utility comes from being able to differentiate real things out there than can harm us or be of interest, so a red insect is poisonous and a blue one tastes great.

Now let's make an A.i. that does that… this will be our first A.i, and it is from the metaphorical kind but it can easily be simulated or constructed and programmed.

Our A.i. Is simply a moving box on a grid with 2 photoreceptors, one tuned to the wavelength of the color Blue, and the other to the wavelength of the color Red, the goal is slightly different, the box will advance as long as the next tile is blue, and stop when the tile is red.

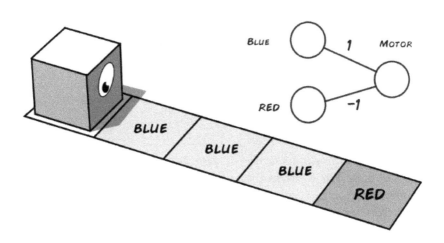

When perceiving a Blue square ahead, the blue photoreceptor generates a binary cyclical signal (the equivalent to a repeating action potential or while condition), and the same thing happens when the red one perceives a red square ahead, when both fire they cancel each other out due to the weights and the Ai stops in a similar way to the Ai crossing the room we previously made.

Now for the interesting part, if one were to code or wire the A.i to differentiate stimuli or perceive when both are present, it would make little sense to wire both stimuli to an integrative intermediate node since then the A.i. wouldn't be able to tell one from the other, let's say we now want to identify a red/blue tile and turn sideways..

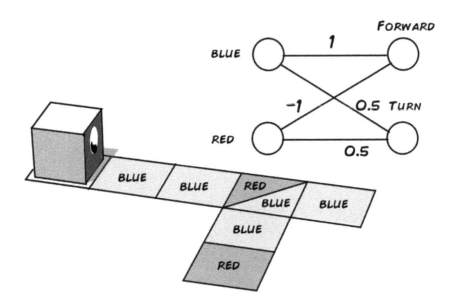

Our NN in this case is a little more complex, there are basically 2 circuits running in parallel, when blue is perceived, both the forward and turn node are targeted, but only the forward one is activated since the weight on the turn node (0.5) is below this neurons threshold (1). To our point, feeling blue or red in this case is simply the experience of the particular networks being activated.

So a parallel arrangement is needed, even though the outputs of our photoreceptors or neurons might converge at some point, the stimuli, in order to be useful needs to be perceived on it's own channel or neuronal circuit, in this case turn and move forward (*There is a strong case for this differentiation happening in the sensory cortex, the brain stem for instance is a converging point and relay.*)

But it all feels so seamless, how can this be ?

There is a cyclic temporal element to consciousness that might be at play in generating such unity, (which we will of course also explore), for now let's just say that 2 stimuli that occur within a sensory cycle (*the length of which is currently unknown and could be variable*) can be perceived as one, this might be considered a side effect of the refresh rate of neuronal circuits that receive inputs from sensory neurons and internal representations in the brain, this we take for granted, experience it as a whole and are continually amazed by this continuity.

If that didn't make sense, think about frames in a movie reel, our visual refresh rate (a resolution fault) constructs seamless movement on screen, while in reality there are individual frames; we can perceive about 10-12 images per second as distinct, more than that and we perceive them as motion.

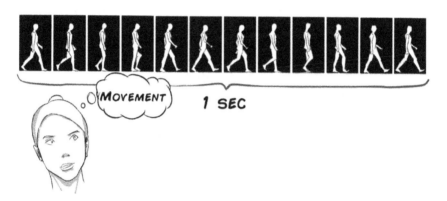

The same mechanism might be at play with the perception of unity in consciousness, that is the refresh rate for perceiving distinct stimuli might be such that 2 stimuli get perceived as one if they happen within the same time frame or are continuous during a smaller interval.

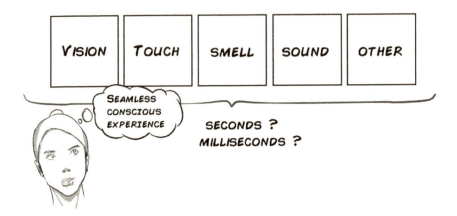

Additionally, intermediate, persistent and parallel processing (all of which are present in the brain), allow for stimuli to be both segregated and experienced as one, but once more we are getting ahead of ourselves, so we'll have to resume this at a later point; for now let's go back to slightly more concrete topics that involve A.i.s…

***

Narrow A.i.s (or why A.i.s fail)

Perhaps the biggest drawback to current A.i.s is that they are not very intelligent beyond a very limited scope (hence the narrow part), don't get me wrong, it is nothing short of amazing that current A.i.s can solve difficult problems like recognizing faces, voices, solving difficult problems that would take us a long time, even coming up with new inventions, it is just that they fail when confronted with our innate level of intelligence.

Let me give you a couple of examples:

Currently there are a number of digital assistants (Siri, Alexa, ok Google, etc, etc), you ask them something and they respond, this is a very specific problem and they are branded as A.i.s, still they sometimes miss the mark in a way akin to Dorothy discovering the wizard of OZ, consider the following interaction:

"Hey digital assistant: Can you translate text on an image ?"

To which the assistant replies :

"Translation- English: text on an image... Spanish: texto en una imagen" !!

If it's not obvious I wanted to know if I could just show it an image with text in another language to translate it (specific A.i.s do exist that can do this), but the digital assistant failed to understand it was a question addressed to itself and its capabilities.

Another common example can be found in pattern recognition which works by rapidly consulting thousands of data points or the algorithm constructed from a training set to determine if a subject is something or other, such an algorithm can be fooled easily by presenting it with a constructed or nonsensical arrangement, consider these 2 images of a camera which an A.i can be fooled with:

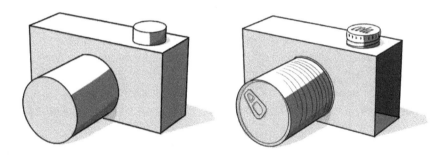

The first one could be made out of clay for all we know, things like texture, detail and context would help here, but A.I.s for the most part ignore these aspects, the second one is an impostor, but without several other concepts we call common sense, the A.i is easily fooled.

So what's missing ?

Well, quite a few things, both of our examples are basically complex database queries; the solution then would be to expand the database to include the missing bits, unfortunately that would not be very efficient since a new query or arrangement would again fool the A.i. ; what we would need is what is called a General A.i., one which closely emulates the way a brain works for which consciousness I believe is a key ingredient.

General A.i.s

In contrast with narrow or weak A.i.s, a general A.i.would not be stumped by context in questions, a general A.i. could understand the concept of self, learn, remember and in general be able to emulate most of the cognitive abilities of humans we already mentioned, a sense of self or consciousness is usually part of these traits, although as noted consciousness and intelligence, even if it's from the general type can overlap or be separate qualities depending on the specific cognitive abilities and neural networks employed.

A General or Strong A.i has yet to be narrowly defined or invented, the best depiction so far can be found in movies and works of fiction (HER, exmachina, the matrix etc, etc), another way to assess a general A.i is through a series of tests, the Turing test for instance where an A.i. Converses with an unsuspecting human and if the human can't tell the difference with another human, the a.i. passes, this level of intelligence has already been achieved (Google's Duplex for instance) yet we are nowhere near a conscious or general Ai, other tests (Wozniak, Goertzel, Nilsson, Severyns) ask of the A.i. to conduct a common human activity successfully to be considered general (enroll in college, make coffee, etc, etc).

These tests I believe are poor metrics for a truly general A.i., for once they can easily be cheated by a purposely built A.i., or in other words, no matter how difficult the task is it can be broken down into a few constituent parts, so I believe that rather than test for generality one could have a better metric by dividing general A.i. into cognitive constituent parts, measuring each one against certain benchmarks and perhaps having a meta test that would then be described as a general A.i. test; we will do just that in part 2 when we try dividing the brain into cognitive functions, neural networks and artificial analogs.

***

Conscious A.i.s

In contrast with other types of AIs, a conscious A.i.,(*the subject of this book*) is not required to perform a human activity or be indistinct in some aspect from humans, some overlap does exist here, but I just want to note that General A.i.s, Narrow A.i.s and Conscious A.i.s are 3 separate things, a 4th distinction arises from the term *Artificial Consciousness*, the specific difference being that it is just an artificial construct that posses consciousness rather than intelligence or intelligence and consciousness. By necessity a C.A.I. will possess artificial consciousness and be an A.i. and can be either narrow or general.

Terms will surely evolve and be replaced with time, for now they are just placeholders for unknown defined functions.

So what is a Conscious A.i. anyways ?

We could start describing a conscious A.i by perhaps it's most apparent quality, it would require a sense of awareness, such awareness can range from a basic awareness of it's environment and it's relationship to it, but what we would ideally want is a deeper understanding of the self as related to other beings (*I am an A.i. there are people, things and animals around me*) or self awareness and a richer understanding of the environment given by general knowledge. (*I can interact with the environment, I exist*).

Such a C.A.i would need to emulate some basic elements or cognitive abilities found in humans, we really don't have anywhere else to look for concepts to emulate, so these can serve as a rough outline towards a stack of elements needed in both biological beings and artificial constructs:

***

Awareness & Simple Self Awareness

At its core, the concept of awareness revolves around perceiving the environment through sensory neurons connected to the outside (*exteroception*), we can speculate that organisms that perceive the environment have a better chance of survival and reproduction, we can also speculate that this could have been one of the first occurrences of awareness in the evolutionary tree, the alternative being to blindly wander about, which would leave finding food, safety and potential mates entirely to chance, a strategy that does happen in nature, but seems rather limiting.

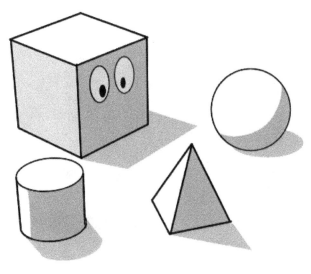

EXTEROCEPTION

Organisms that additionally are capable of awareness of the internal state of the body (*interoception*) can also be considered to have an evolutionary advantage, imagine for instance being injured and not being able to tell where you were injured, the injury could easily get worse to the point of incapacitating you, such is the purpose of pain, being hungry is another type of internal awareness, once more this mechanism seems to subserve basic and defined goals like survival and reproduction and can be considered a first or basic type of self awareness.

INTEROCEPTION

A second type of basic self awareness is the one where you can sense or perceive where your body parts are in relationship to yourself or the environment (*propioception*), once more there is an evolutionary advantage, knowing where you are in relationship with a dangerous cliff, food or mate is helpful.

PROPIOCEPTION

Perceiving the environment, oneself (*as it relates to ones function, performance or homeostasis*) and the self in relationship to the environment are all currently achievable, mainly in the field of robotics, but narrow A.i.s also poses some scripted or hard coded variations.

Rich Awareness, Rich Self Awareness

When people mention self awareness, they are usually not referring to the fact that you can be aware of your inner temperature, the occasional bowel movement or where your arm is resting, what most people have in mind is the awareness of one as being a distinct entity or person existing in the world, today, in this moment and through time, both past and future. We can call this a sense of *rich self awareness* to differentiate it from the previously mentioned basic or simple self awareness.

Dissecting this concept brings forth new realizations and insights, mainly that in order to sustain the awareness of one as an independent entity we at least need to have the cognitive ability to form and hold knowledge (in this case the knowledge that we exist), the second and closely tied cognitive ability needed would be the capacity to learn new things and recall them, or memory.

Once these building blocks are in place, we can evolve our awareness of self with the concept of time and place which we can now acquire and hold, allowing us to reflect on our self through time and space.

We can expect more complexity if we wish to recreate this type of awareness since new systems operating at the same time are now needed.

Rich Awareness or Social Awareness.

One last type of awareness we need to mention is that of others, not only as things out there in the environment, but as related to us as fellow beings that are also self aware or not.

Communication, language and more complex concepts and ideas come into play here.

Current A.i.s lack both Rich Self Awareness and Rich or Social Awareness, although some elements of both can be found in certain programs, a scheduling program for instance knows about time, and complex communications in between programs is commonplace, what is missing is fine-tuning the details and creating a purpose built system that encompasses all these disparate elements, let's briefly review the addition-al (*constituent*) elements of the awareness we just mentioned.

Emotions, emotional awareness.

Please review the chapter on emotions for an overview...

Emotions are uniquely biological, and perhaps only applicable to a subset of animals and humans, explaining emotions within the concept of awareness is a little challenging due to the interconnected and goal oriented nature of emotions, we can simplify by wedging emotional awareness in between memory and simple awareness, we also need to add some unconscious processes and a dash of networking, just like cooking...

The business of awareness is perceiving phenomena, both internal and external, so the first thing to note is that emotions can be perceived by the individual, this perception which we are all very aware of can come in many forms, a sudden attack of laughter, sadness or fear for instance, unlike interoception though, there is a higher order of processing that is happening here, one that by and large we can't stop or modify, hence the unconscious part, and that is based on previous experience and instinctu-al behavior, we can again simplify by grouping these two under memory.

In play, emotions (*also the more immediate feelings*) are responses to internal and external stimuli and their processing (usually around some baseline level) , hunger for instance (*I feel hungry, I am aware I am hungry*) aggregates unconscious stimuli: levels of nutrients, neural signals, hor-mones; and packages them into a cocktail of neurotransmitters in certain neural networks we experience as hunger; sadness and other more complex emotions pull (combine elements) from memory and complex processing, yet seems to result in another chemical cocktail that we experience as sadness: loss, a precursor or cause of sadness for instance requires a number of higher capacity functions, mainly the capacity of the organism to store in memory something, attach positive emotions to it and then be aware that it's been lost, an internal response is then generated without the organisms conscious involvement until the experi-ence of sadness is registered.

***

Memory

Memory like consciousness is not an unitary or simple concept as previously mentioned, but can be understood at its core as the recollection of past events, stimuli or behavior, importantly we can be aware or not of this recollection; to the organism it is incredibly useful, for instance it allows classification and discrimination, imagine that something is harmful to you, rather than repeating the bad experience over and over you can now avoid it, finding a source of food and remembering the location of it also helps with survival, discriminating for pray, predator and potential partner increases your reproduction and survival odds, and although most of what we consider memory is conscious (I.e. we are aware of the recollection or learning), unconscious memory (or implicit memory) also exists and helps us in other ways like muscle memory and priming.

Consult the overview of memory in the previous chapters for the basics, as related to consciousness and awareness, memory is a prerequisite for knowledge, importantly the knowledge of ones existence and past events involving oneself, without it we would forever be stuck in a state of being without knowing who we are, some amnesiac patients suffer (or enjoy) this state to a certain degree and perhaps some animals experience something similar.

The good news is that memory in A.i.s is something quite achievable, even memory related to the self is quite common albeit in its simpler form, like recording where a robotic arms has been, or what series of steps have been taken, sometimes thousands. Unfortunately a deeper understanding or awareness of one self requires a different type of memory, a rich one related to facts and events, as well as integration with other aspects, here is where knowledge and learning comes into play.

Learning and Knowledge

Both learning and knowledge are intimately related with memory and consciousness, self awareness is thought to be attained after acquiring basic concepts about the self, things like learning about the environment and ones relationship with it, followed by higher concepts of entities out there that are both different and similar to one.

In infants for instance memory develops at around the 1 year mark, but self awareness is believed to surface after another year or so culminating at around the 8 year mark for a fully formed idea of the self, we can expect a newborn to be conscious in the basic awareness type we discussed previously, yet like mentioned this is a gradual affair with multiple steps that involves learning and recalling memories first to then progress to a richer awareness followed by rich self awareness.

Self concept and self reference

A concept or idea can be understood in simple biological terms as connections in between disparate neuronal assemblies that represent stimuli or other concepts and ideas, this in itself is a vaguely understood mechanism but remarkable non the less. Relevant here is the concept needed for self awareness, or self-concept... Self concept is the representation of the self or entity from an outside point of view or second person, and represents the idea that one is different from other entities out there which have certain related properties; once this concept is in place (in the infant elements appear as early as ~3 months old), self reference can then occur for instance, the use of *I, Mine, my.*

Simple organisms and A.i.s can acquire and hold knowledge, it could be hereditary, learned or passed on as a set of simple instructions, but once more what we are after is specific knowledge about the self tied to past events, an A.i would need to develop rich self awareness trough components capable of self concepts and self reference, and most likely the apparatus to generate new concepts and their integration would need to be in place beforehand, learning in ANN does seem to fit the bill here, or at least a nascent version of it, yet the narrow domain ANN serve does not help; for instance, an ANN can learn it's own performance on a tomato sorting job and then reference this result to improve in further trials, yet it will never know what a tomato is, or that it is a machine devoted to sorting them, the capability to hold other seemingly irrelevant pieces of information and bringing them together was not given to it.

***

Attention

It might not seem apparent to you, but you are constantly filtering the world around you and are only really aware of a small (perhaps tiny) fraction of it, our brains have evolved to make do with processing and space limitations while at the same time providing us with a fine level of detail and specificity when needed, this cognitive mechanism is usually given the name of attention or enthrallment.

You know the drill; attention like memory, consciousness and other cognitive topics is not a unitary, simple or agreed upon process, at this stage it is worth noting that attention doesn't seem to be strictly necessary for the process of consciousness to arise since attention deals mostly with having a limited capacity for perceiving and processing stimuli and the allocation of mental resources to them, strictly speaking though attention can also be synonymous with awareness either conscious or unconscious, but here we focus on the former process, attention plays several roles in consciousness and is of interest both for understanding some thorny aspects of Artificial Consciousness like free will and of great interest for practical applications.

Some relevant aspects related to attention we might want to be aware (*for later emulation*):

- Attention seems to operate by diving a set amount of mental real estate into smaller allocations with less resolution, some of this allocation can be concurrent (*like multitasking*) and it can also be maintained with effort (*concentration*).

- Attention can be directed, this direction can either be top down, that is initiated or maintained from within (*as in I am paying attention to this thing that is of interest to me*) or bottom up, that is initiated or maintained from the outside (*that thing outside there demands my attention*). It can also be internal (*mentally paying attention to some idea*) or external, *focusing your gaze on something of interest.*

- We can attend to a great variety of stimuli both external and internal including concepts and subjects related to the self (or self reflection).

- Attention and Memory are closely tied together via working memory: a mental buffer that holds things in a temporal space and can be directed via attention; additionally, things we pay attention to have a greater chance of being remembered later.

If there is one other aspect (*besides consciousness*) where computers and current A.i.s falter, is attention, while the mechanisms might be complex, they can surely be emulated, the reason I believe current A.i.s are poor where it comes to attention is both a lack of sophisticated autonomy or agency and also perhaps (*and paradoxically*) an overabundance of computational resources, (why recreate or use a limited schema when computational resources and storage are cheap); Current examples of artificial attention are pick and place robots and pattern recognition software (face, object, voice, etc ,etc).

***

Language, communication & inner worlds.

Like attention, language is probably not strictly necessary for consciousness, yet it sits on top of the stack so far discussed and can be found along the ladder of awareness in the form of entities communicating in a number of ways, from simple programmed behaviors in between animals as simple as worms, to the complex communication of inner thoughts and ideas through agreed upon learned language found in humans.

As it pertains to consciousness, inner speech (*the voice in your head*)

allows us to reflect privately on experiences and thoughts, and is perhaps the ultimate form of self consciousness we can achieve, a little auditory private world all of our own we can both initiate and listen to, in this respect language achieves it's most basic form in the way or manner of stimuli encoded in a specific way and stored for future representation and processing.

There is also a visual equivalent and multimodal capabilities (taste, texture, etc) are possible and what we group and call imagination.

While communication is commonplace in between A.i.s, language, let alone a proprietary agreed upon language is not. Inner representations of stimuli exist in some A.i.s although they fall into the narrow a.i. side of things, a multimodal inner representation is still lacking along with imagination and the aforementioned relationship to the self.

Break - Story Time

At some point in my life I used to work as a food runner in a very busy and popular restaurant in San Francisco, my job description was simply to deliver the correct food to the right table and seat (*we had something like 100 numbered seats so it was a little daunting at first*). My real job though consisted on being a sort of translator and peace keeper in between the servers (mostly white and focused on getting drunk and taking orders) and the kitchen (mostly latinos and focused on getting drunk and cooking), a fun recipe for mayhem if you ask me. Being a fluent speaker of both Spanish and English,(*and sticking to coffee*) I think I did an ok job and counted friends and foes in both trenches.

Even though we weren't given free food at the end of our shifts, we were given a 50% discount, so I ended up trying each one of the 30 or so dishes on the menu, most were quite good, but I settled on the braised short ribs as my favorite even though I was mostly vegetarian, it was that good, and was reserved for special occasions only.

After a particular chaotic shift one day, I rewarded myself with my favorite dish, upon handing my order ticket to the kitchen, one of the cooks I had helped during my shift asked me if I wanted them (the short ribs) cooked in any specific way, having studied this dish for a while, I was well prepared for the answer and asked for a specific cooking level, amount of mashed potatoes and gravy, the cook smiled.

What came out of this little arrangement was the most memorable thing I have ever eaten and probably will, it was spectacular, I also learned a very important lesson that day, one that is applicable here.

Like food, consciousness can be separated into multiple constituent parts, but simply throwing them into a pot or pan and stirring won't make a dish, trial and error is required and if you want to have a really memorable dish or recreate consciousness artificially, a great deal of attention into how the elements fit together (and maybe some luck and love) is needed, we will start piecing the parts in a later book, for now, let's turn our attention to some important odds and ends worth mentioning.

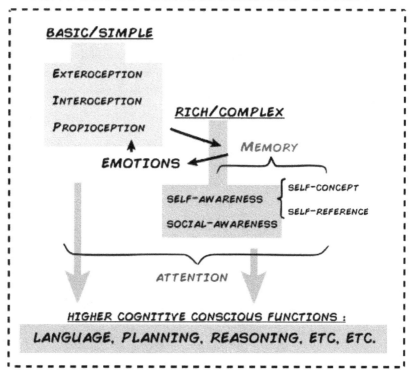

Before leaving this section, here is a grouping of the basic elements or ingredients of consciousness we've been mentioning, from top to bottom, simple to complex, a stack or mini recipe if you will.

***

Intelligence in C.A.I.

Artificial Consciousness and Conscious Artificial Intelligence have a subtle distinction; while we might recreate consciousness trough emulating a set of cognitive abilities or coming up with new analogs, it is the end application where this distinction might arise, consider 2 new types of artificial constructs:

Our first artificial construct would be self aware and capable of inner thoughts, complex language and all the elements listed before, yet it might not be intelligent, since well, intelligence presupposes some kind of goal or challenge and the means to surpass it or find a solution.

Our second one, would additionally have some problem to solve and thus can be named a Conscious Artificial Intelligence (or C.A.I.). It is still not clear if such distinction is critical for recreating consciousness or sustaining it, for most of our cognitive functions are believed to serve our biological needs, we'll expand below when talking about artificial goals, for now it is sufficient to know that this distinction exists.

I EXIST TO
SOLVE PROBLEMS

***

Curiosity

Humans (and other animals) are naturally curious beings; during the early phases of life it is theorized that curiosity is a way to train ourselves by way of interacting with the world, memorizing responses and building a knowledge base of sorts, at the neuronal level it is believed we start out with a fully unpruned tree of connections and through experience (driven by the environment and in part curiosity) some connections get lost while others survive or get reinforced. The behavior does persist throughout our lives and is helpful in discovering new solutions to problems and a driver for creativity.

Curiosity (along memory, training and a knowledge base) might play a crucial role in the design of a C.A.i., so far most of our A.i.s are trained with specific datasets or stimuli thanks in part to the narrow aspect, (A neural network whose job is to detect tumors is not given a dataset to detect bananas).

A C.A.i. or a predecessor to a C.A.i will surely benefit from the capacity to explore and learn on it's own.

***

Virtual, Artificial or Biological ?

Can an artificial consciousness be made out of non biological elements or does it need to be biological, and can it be virtual or merely artificial ?

There are currently 2 schools of thought about this subject, on one hand there are those that believe that by reducing the constituent parts found in the brain, that is connections, neurons and computations (sometimes called the Neural Correlates of Consciousness or NCC) and later recreating them either artificially or virtually, we can recreate consciousness.(Also called *Functionalism*)

A second posture is that consciousness is a quality that demands either a physical system (this would rule out virtual consciousness) or strictly a human one.

We as species have a poor track record of accepting evidence and facts, so even though I believe there is enough evidence (but no working Artificial consciousness) to rule out the second premise, a considerable amount of time will be needed before this is common knowledge, additionally if you believe that humans poses some extra dimensional quality granted by the divine, no amount of theory or even a C.A.i that tells you it is conscious might suffice or matter, such has been our nature in the past.

How about the distinction in between virtual vs artificial ?

By artificial here we mean that an A.i could be created with man made parts, it could be gears, pistons, switches or any other means, such construct would interact with the physical world as we know it.

Artificial/ mechanical A.i. Interacting with the real world.

In contrast, a virtual A.i. interacts with virtual stimuli regardless of how it's made, the A.i. is also virtual (neurons simulated on a computer), although it can also be of a more mechanical nature and interact with a virtual space.

Virtual A.i. Interacting with a virtual world

If for instance you (A biological intelligence) interacts with a video game or program (a virtual stimuli) does your experience, qualia or consciousness disappear ? It most likely doesn't (*I hope*) , it might be of a different nature, but it's still an internal representation.

At the bottom of these 2 flavors of A.i.implementation, what we really are trying to do is recreate computations and their results, for the purpose of our discussion that is enough. If a virtual, artificial or biological construct processes stimuli, virtual or real (*physical*) and comes up with the same response or process we can consider them equals.

And why bring this up ?

Well, we are in the business of recreating consciousness and applying that towards a goal (or C.A.i), so we now have a few routes to consider while building or experimenting:

- Artificial construct, real environment. (like robotics)
- Artificial construct, virtual environment. (Virtually testing physical sensors)
- Virtual construct, Virtual Environment.(probably most efficient)
- Virtual construct, real environment (challenging but novel)

In reality, elements of all might be present in A.I.s, and C.A.I.s for the foreseeable future.

***

Free Will

Are we really in control of our actions ? If we are recreating consciousness, is this control a property of consciousness or do we also need to somehow recreate it? Again some difficult to answer questions that in some way or other we've been asking since we could ask questions and chose to do so...

There are ample schools of thought about what is free will and to what degree we are capable of it, A good top down definition of free will in general can be considered the capacity of choice (taking one of a number of available paths for instance) in which the outcome has not been determined by past events, the degree then revolves around what capacity of choice we can have and what events have not been determined for us beforehand, it's somehow redundant if we define it this way though, so let's dig a bit deeper.

Consciousness plays a role in as much as the stimuli and memories present us with a current course of action or choice based on our main goals of survival and reproduction, It plays a role rather than the full part due to how our memories interact with our conscious decisions, that is they seem to be 2 different systems working at times in parallel rather than always in a sequential manner, sometimes memories bypass consciousness and we end up not knowing why we took the decision, but to the outside world it is the entity (us) who ultimately took the decision.

To complicate matters more, decisions are rarely binary and the results aren't always known or certain, it might be a deterministic environment, but information is not always complete, so I believe our free will, and free will we might develop artificially will follow a narrow path of behavior dictated by primary goals and incomplete information.

Another way of looking at free will is via our innate limitations, are we free to spend a couple of hours underwater holding our breadth ? Can we freely gravitate above the ground ? These type of nonsensical questions apply to us humans, but might not apply to other species, so freedom of action has variable limits defined by both the environment and our innate or acquired capabilities, it is not too unreasonable to think that this situation extends to other domains, so for instance behavior and inner representations (aka thoughts and feelings) might also have a limit based on what we have experienced and our nature, choice then is relegated to which network or system is primed to respond first to certain stimuli, that's not to say that we can't randomly choose in between 2 unknown or equally weighted options , something most of us struggle with and call indecision.

***

Artificial Goals ?

We've been talking about the importance of goals in biological systems

137

as evolutionary tools that direct both cognitive evolution and ultimately behavior, but how about artificial constructs, would they also need goals to emulate our cognitive abilities ? If so which goals ? Is this important for consciousness at all?

The answer to the first question, (do we need goals ?) I believe is a graded and definitive maybe, current A.I.s all employ some kind of goal, it could be solving a problem or detecting a pattern for instance, we could remove this goal and end up with a meaningless piece of code or artifact, yet if we were to recreate consciousness and self awareness, it is unclear this construct would be meaningless if stripped out if it's goals, this is a bit hard to describe, because well it doesn't exist yet, but could in theory be constructed if we manage to fully emulate consciousness.

We are on more solid ground when we use goals, at the bare minimum we know they coexist with consciousness and evolution tells us they are a soft requirement, they also provide us with some needed direction while testing out new A.i.s and ultimately have proven to be quite useful to advance technology.

So goals are mostly needed, but perhaps not an absolute requirement, but which goals ?

Our primary goals are reproduction and survival, but if we look closer we can boil it down to survival, since reproduction can be considered a means to survive in a longer timespan, or in other words if you lifespan was infinite reproduction wouldn't be that much of pressing issue.

By removing reproduction from our C.A.i. goal requirements, we can now focus on survival, the thing is survival is also a non issue, or at least a less complex requirement, a C.A.i will for the foreseeable future be under our tutelage, we humans will provide the power, code and environment, at least initially, thinking too far ahead is on the realm of science fiction (the last part of this series). For now, we can use intermediate goals in the form of those goals that are specific to a certain cognitive ability we are trying to emulate (like pattern recognition, pattern recall, etc, etc).

***

Conclusions & Findings

A probably imperfect but hopefully reasonable plan of attack for creating a C.A.i would involve at least 3 parts: an overview of the problem along with basic concepts to serve as a common ground (this book) detailing and translating relevant networks into functional components, and finally integrations, applications and general considerations.

We unfortunately don't have much to show yet, but things do look promising, here I present a few findings that will serve as a rough map of the journey ahead, keep in mind that they might or might not hold true in the future, but non the less, they need to be tested and experiments and theories generated with them.

1. Consciousness is the subjective and variable integration of external and internal stimuli by an agent into a cohesive whole or part that subsists during a period of time in space.

Experimental path: Integrate environmental and internal information into an artificial construct capable of such things.

Comments: This could be trivial to implement in a naive way, but rather challenging if we emulate nature and use just a few elements, circuits and connection schemas, implicit in this theory is the notion that consciousness is not the sole domain of humans, primates or even biological beings, hence the word agent, although the experience and particulars of each entity along with their class might be, implicit also is the transient nature of consciousness we discussed when we went over the black bars.

2. Branching from this simple concept, we can further define other types of consciousness like self consciousness, rich consciousness   and

subconsciousness.

3. These additional divisions require additional functions and capabilities, mainly memory and related subsystems (information integration and interplay for instance), parallelism in between dedicated subsystems and the ability to create, hold and update concepts, but other elements might be needed as well.

Experimental path: Isolate brain networks and specific neural circuits relevant to each conscious modality and cognitive behavior, recreate and integrate them, note that some might not be strictly needed but at this point it is unknown, some simplification and probably a liberal interpretation of certain mechanisms and their replacement by more efficient or practical ones is to be expected.

Comments: I believe this is the hardest part, we probably are looking at hundreds or a couple of thousand different networks and systems (local, global, interconnected) out of which picking the relevant ones for a barebones implementation could be a long journey, we also lack detailed biological maps.

4.Goals and emotions seem to be a hard requirement for human consciousness, mostly due to evolutionary aspects, but they might not be needed for Artificial consciousness in a strict sense, still, they seem to be a requirement for a C.A.I.

Experimental path: Provide artificial or real goals and emotions, the alternative being to bootstrap biological needs, goals and emotions or remove them altogether, there's a bit of semantics at play here as well, we could also state that one goal of a conscious construct is to understand goals and then define emotions as the internal signal of how close or far from this goal the construct is.

Comments: It is yet unclear which requirements are needed or even if they are needed at all, the ideal is a general intelligence that can be given any goal and understands both context and can come up with it's own solutions through self directed learning and problem solving, but once again this seems to be out of reach for now and we might have to settle for the best next thing, a basic implementation of consciousness after which we can start incorporating higher goals and even emotions.

5. As it concerns to current A.i.s, specifically popular implementations of A.i.s; consciousness is not present as we understand it on biological or human terms yet there seems to be enough of the elements needed to recreate a basic one.

Comments: Many aspects of a theoretical C.A.I. exist in software or hardware form, it doesn't seem to be a strictly technical issue by itself, that is the individual components are available or could be created with some effort, rather it seems to an issue of integrating these components in the right order, if you've been following the cooking analogy, the raw ingredients are mostly there, a chef or chefs to make it happen and the vision to recreate the dish is what's missing…

***

While writing this first part the Wright Brothers and their inaugural flights during the 1900's frequently popped into my mind, think about it for a second, previous to those first flights man had already gotten it into his head that man made flight was not only possible, but had tried many ways to achieve it, sometimes even succeeding, from emulating wing flapping to using lighter than air balloons, now a days it is easy to find these ideas quaint and their mistakes obvious, birds are incredibly light and the movement through air of an airfoil generates lift, this is somehow common knowledge, but back in those days it took a lot of trial and error. As it regards to consciousness and artificial consciousness we are in those days.

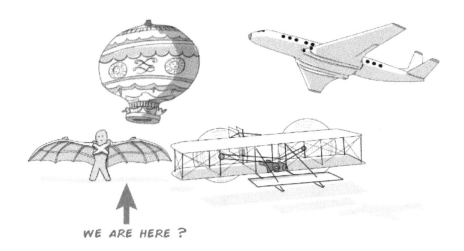

WE ARE HERE ?

Like in those days we know what we want (flight, consciousness) but are not entirely sure how to achieve it, and our first tries while laudable, interesting and even productive have not gotten us there, we also lack the precise details of what makes consciousness stick and how to apply it to our advantage in the form of a C.A.i.

Least we end up in a sour note here, I would like to go back to where we started, me fainting while trying to reach a ringing phone while I was a kid.

If there's anything that is worth remembering after all these words, is that black bar that occurred during those seconds while I was gone, that time when we are not here due to sleep or injury, that nothingness that occurs before we live, and that void that seemingly happens again when we cease to exist, what is important for us is the space in between, when out of nothing we, biology, evolution, superstition and all create and experience something, that is worth not only understanding but also recreating, and so we must go forth like others before,I believe that is something truly meaningful, on par with experiencing it all in peace and harmony with each other…

*****

Bibliography & suggested reading:

Basic or introductory texts on Neuroscience and Ai:

Purves, Dale, et al. Neuroscience. Sinauer Associates, 2018.

Gazzaniga, Michael S., et al. Cognitive Neuroscience: the Biology of the Mind. W.W. Norton & Company, 2019.

Russell, Stuart Jonathan, and Peter Norvig. Artificial Intelligence: a Modern Approach. Pearson, 2018.

Networks, Cycles & Consciousness:

Buzsáki, G. Rhythms of the Brain. Oxford University Press, 2011.

Sporns, Olaf. Networks of the Brain. Mit Press, 2016.

Koch, Christof. The Quest for Consciousness: a Neurobiological Approach. Roberts and Co., 2004.

Memory Related:

Tulving, Endel. The Oxford Handbook of Memory. Oxford Univ. Press, 2010.

Kandel, Eric R. In Search of Memory The Emergence of a New Science of Mind. Paw Prints, 2008.

Gluck, Mark A., and Catherine E. Myers. Gateway to Memory: an Introduction to Neural Network Modeling of the Hippocampus and Learning. London, 2001.

Squire, Larry R., and Eric R. Kandel. Memory: from Mind to Molecules. Roberts & Co., 2009.

Domain specific:

Feynman, Richard Phillips, et al. Six Easy Pieces Essentials of Physics Explained by Its Most Brilliant Teacher. Basic, 2011.

Bergstrom, Carl T., and Lee Alan Dugatkin. Evolution. W.W. Norton & Company, 2016.

Lewis, Penelope A. The Secret World of Sleep: the Surprising Science of the Mind at Rest. St. Martin's Griffin, 2014.

Kemmerer, David L. Cognitive Neuroscience of Language. Psychology Press, 2015.

Miller, Bruce L., and Jeffrey L. Cummings. The Human Frontal Lobes: Functions and Disorders. The Guilford Press, 2018.

Marr, David. Vision: a Computational Investigation into the Human Representation and Processing of Visual Information. MIT Press, 2010.